INCREDIBLE WOMEN ON HOW TO EMBRACE EQUITY

GLOBAL INFLUENCERS PUBLISHING HOUSE
152 Prince Charles Cr, #17-12 Singapore 159013
Website: www.globalinfluencers.sg
Email: shikha@globalinfluencers.sg
First Published in Singapore by
Global Influencers Publishing House 2023

Title: Redefining the Rules - Incredible Women
on How to Embrace Equity
ISBN: 978-981-18-6621-0

GLOBAL INFLUENCERS PUBLISHING HOUSE

Redefining The Rules

INCREDIBLE WOMEN ON HOW TO EMBRACE EQUITY

Contents

Preface

At the school year's beginning, a first-grade teacher takes a bunch of sticky plasters with colourful cartoons. "We are going to play a pretend game," she tells her young pupils. "Imagine you've hurt yourself somewhere, and I've got these nice plasters to put on your wound," she says in her distinctive first-grade teacher voice, filled with excitement, whilst showing what are probably the coolest plasters for six-year-olds.

She calls one child to the front of the classroom and asks where it hurts. "Here," says the first child, holding up their index finger to show a pretend cut on the tip of it. The teacher puts the plaster there. When the first child has been cared for and, as a result, beams with joy, she starts walking around the classroom, and no matter where the other children say they have pain, they get a plaster on the same spot as the first child – on the same tip of their left index finger.[1]

It isn't hard to imagine the children protesting, "That's not fair!" and, "But I hurt my knee!" – or arm, or nose – whilst pointing to the diverse areas where they have pretended injuries.

Every kid in that classroom experienced that putting a plaster on a spot where you are perfectly healthy doesn't do

---

[1]Niaura, D. (2019). "Teacher Uses Band-Aids To Explain Difference Between Equality Vs Equity, Eight-Year-Olds Understand It Better Than Adults". *Bored Panda*. https://www.boredpanda.com/equality-equity-band-aid-student-lesson/

good, and neither does it help alleviate the pain. The teacher showed the kids that we all have different needs and gave an excellent demonstration of equity that gives her the freedom to respond to her pupils' individual needs throughout the school year.

Equality means treating everyone equally, and everybody gets the same. In this case, a plaster on their index finger, regardless of where they had pain. Equity, on the other hand, means giving people what they truly need – putting the plaster where it hurts. The teacher has prevented the kids from whining, "But he made a 'great effort' although he has more mistakes than me".

The following picture explains the difference between equity and equality better than a thousand words. When we are given the same, we can't all succeed, because we all have different skills and abilities, wants and needs.

Image: https://dividedwefall.org/

Equality is often not fair. Fairness is focusing on equity and responding to Everyone's *individual* needs.

Most societies, and corporations, tend to be based on equality rather than equity. We give everyone the same training programme and opportunities to apply for the same jobs. Most companies ask everyone to work the same or at least similar hours.

However, if a highly qualified person lacks confidence as a leader, why not provide an individual coaching programme to build their confidence and enable them to show up as strong leaders? Suppose a potential leadership candidate doesn't have the industry connections required for a job. Why not assign a mentor who can open doors or send them to the right industry conferences and invite them to the right meetings? If a parent needs to attend school meetings in the late afternoon, why not allow them the flexibility to go? If women lack the confidence that they can be leaders, why not create a safe space for women to find their way in a male-dominated world by sending them to Women in Leadership programmes?

Companies often state their commitment to "Diversity, Equity and Inclusion" without understanding what Equity requires. Equity is a notion that is very difficult for organisations to embrace. "We take the best person for the job" is what I hear in almost every organisation I work with as a consultant. You might even have said or thought this.

"We take the best person for the job" is wrong for various reasons.

First, we tend to measure job candidates on male perceptions of what the best candidate looks like, whether it is through the wording of the job advertisement or because the interviewer is male and, of course, likes to recruit people with a similar demographic background. Our biases attract us to sameness, and it's easier to deal with people like us. We may ignore that skills such as "compassionate", team player", and "reflective" are excellent characteristics for the leadership position we are trying to fill.

Second, we may assume that the position needs travel, and a woman with small children doesn't want to travel. We could take a different perspective and ask whether the position requires that much travelling. And, very importantly: we could ask the young mother whether she would like to travel for work.

Third, we could shift our perspective and ask who would be the best person for the *company* – rather than for the job. Diversity increases group intelligence. We all stand to benefit from diversity because different perspectives are included, which can lead to innovation.

For companies, this benefit translates into nine percentage points of additional Earnings Before Interest and Taxes (EBIT). Isn't it highly likely that hiring a brown woman into a white male leadership team brings an innovation advantage to the company? The slightly lower qualification of the "diverse" candidate may get you a handsome financial benefit.

Fourth, research shows that women often undersell themselves. The woman may be more suitable if you have two equally qualified candidates. Also, from my experience, a woman usually has to prove herself repeatedly before getting promoted, and a misstep is often looked at more negatively. Think about it: a woman who loses her temper may be branded hysterical. It quickly turns into a negative character description. A man who loses his temper is just a male colleague.

That the woman had to work harder to get to the same place as a man again gives you a reason to hire her rather than him.

Finally, confidence, which we often hire for, is more prevalent in men but does not correlate with competence, as research shows. But it does trick us into believing he is the "best person for the job".

Or should we say – unless we take conscious measures to avoid this cocktail of biases – we will take "the best man for the job".

This is just one example of how most organisations do not practice equity. Our society can do with much more understanding of and commitment to equity.

This book explores what Equity means so that societies can become genuinely equitable. With 17 authors sharing very different experiences and perspectives, we hope to provide you with plenty of inspiration and food for thought on what we can do to make the world fairer.

Let's all embrace equity for a place that allows all genders to be the best version of themselves and lead the lives they deserve.

METTE JOHANSSON

Founder and Chair, KeyNote Women Speakers
Award-Winning Entrepreneur, Speaker,
Author, Consultant, Facilitator and Coach

STORY ONE

The Turtle, the Rabbit, and the Level Playing Field

Redesign the terrain to leverage the unique strengths of diversity.

Many think equity is levelling the playing field. I believe equity cannot be guaranteed just by levelling the playing field. We are not all running the same race, even if the distance is the same. Regardless of the "level" of the field, insurmountable barriers can prevent an equitable race.

Speaking of inequitable races, remember that old story about the Rabbit and Turtle? You know, the one where the rabbit challenges the turtle to a running race. The rabbit starts strong but then gets complacent and cocky and goes off to sleep under a tree. The diligent turtle continues to plod along and manages to win. The moral of the story is – slow and steady wins the race.

But what would the story look like if the rabbit hadn't gotten complacent? Chances are that the rabbit would've won hands down with minimal effort – because fast and steady ALWAYS wins the race on terra firma. And there is little "talent" required on the part of the rabbit because the terrain is designed to play to its strengths. For the turtle, on the other hand – the likelihood of its winning is pretty low – no matter how much it "keeps going", "keeps its head in the game", "stays focused", "never gives up", or whatever other motivational quote you can think of. And the reason is – the terrain itself is not letting the turtle play to its strengths. It is not a terrain designed for the turtle to succeed.

Even against these odds, the ultra-motivated turtle might try to win by being more like the rabbit. It may try to "fit in" by changing its appearance or behaviours. It even might accept being paid less than the rabbit for doing the same job – just to have a chance to win. By being diligent and focused, the turtle might start winning, and by some miracle, it might get ahead of other rabbits. But sadly, even then, it will not be accepted into the rabbit's club. The turtle will always be an outsider – a "wannabe" rabbit. In fact, when the turtle starts behaving like the rabbit, it will be penalised for doing the same things. The turtle just cannot win.

A clear parallel to this story is being a woman in the workplace. You see, I was that proverbial steady turtle – who joined the rabbit race in the late 90s. Throughout school and college, I excelled academically and never considered myself lesser than my male counterparts. At home, I had the most supportive family – who told me that if I put in the hard work, I would be unstoppable. I could win.

Armed with a degree from a premier college, filled with enthusiasm, and ready to give it my best, I joined the ranks of working women in the late 90s. I learnt quickly that even having the same degree as my male colleagues did not get me the same respect.

Picture this – several corporate colleagues are gathered in the conference room of a high-rise building, and there is a big marketing project to be briefed on. I am one of the new hires and happen to be the only female in the room. The senior director in the room looks at me purposefully. Inwardly, I am delighted to be the "chosen one". The delight is short-lived. I hear him say casually, "Go arrange coffee for all of us. And while you're at it, get these documents photocopied as well".

I am in shock, but I Don't say a word in the spirit of doing what needs to be done. I dutifully get on with it. I wish I could say this was a one-off. Sadly, various iterations of the same scenario continued throughout my initial career.

The "busy work", the things the men didn't want to do, would always flow to me. Need to arrange a "cultural event" – Priya will do it. Need to "babysit" the interns, "Priya – take care of it". Need to organise a team lunch – "Priya, you get it done". And all this was on top of my "day job". And needless to say, when the time came for annual appraisals, none of these extra-curriculars benefitted me. It was a thankless job.

Like the diligent turtle I was, though, I continued to plod along and made steady progress. I had to work twice as hard and deliver twice as much as some of my male counterparts just to be gauged on par with them. And so deep was my conditioning that I didn't blink. I didn't find it the least bit inequitable – I was just so glad to even be in the race when so many of my fellow female warriors had to drop off.

When I say that the terrain is not designed for us women, I mean it. In the ancient age of hunters and the agricultural period, women had a natural disadvantage in terms of physical strength. On top of that, the inherent biological duties of childbirth and child care meant that women were naturally relegated to the role of homemakers. This would have been fine if the economic value placed on these activities was equal to that of the breadwinner.

The issue was that the breadwinner was seen as the superior contributor to the fabric of the society – economic power was the only power that mattered. In the industrial age, again, women were not given opportunities to participate in the creation of economic value and had to fight for equal rights. Fast forward to the information age, and now the digital age, some of the inherent disadvantages women had were removed – we could argue that the playing field had been levelled. However, some issues persist. The terrain is like a fixed ground where rabbits can excel, but the turtle can't succeed:

- It's a "Privileged Club" – Free for those who can afford it and very expensive for those who can't.
- There is a specific "mould" for what a leader looks like – typically Pale, Male and Stale.
- The rules for the game are that you need to be "always on", with no concept of balance or having a home life.

And this meant that success continued to elude women, no matter how hard they tried.

Research[2] shows that while women join the workforce in almost equal numbers as men, their numbers keep declining over time. And by the time we reach the top of the pyramid, we see a significantly diminished 26% of women in the workforce. Several theories have been postulated about why this happens, but the most common thread is that life gets in the way.

There is a wry saying, "Women are expected to raise kids like they Don't work and work like they Don't have kids". Sadly,

---

[2]LeanIn.Org and McKinsey & Company. (2022). *Women in the Workplace 2022.* https://womenintheworkplace.com (accessed February 1, 2023).

outside the very privileged few, most women are faced with this hard choice. Without reliable and affordable childcare or jobs that can give women the flexibility to manage work and life, women have no choice but to "lean out".

They say no to the post-work drinks where the "real" power play happens, say no to meaty jobs that require travel or relocation, and say no to senior positions that require overtime. And as a result, they fall out of the race.

Their male counterparts, on the other hand, keep going. They are rewarded not only at work but even at home. When they come home as family breadwinners, there is that sense of triumph and exaltation.

Women work equally hard, if not more so, at home. And yet, the value of the work women do – child rearing, running the house, cooking etc. is diminished compared to the economic value of the money earned by the men.

As I said, I was glad to even be in a position to remain in the race. I was lucky to have an amazingly supportive spouse and a system at home that allowed me to pursue my career. But to say it was all hunky-dory would be an overstatement. As I progressed, I discovered that some of the advice I had received in the past did not serve me anymore.

I never considered myself disadvantaged when I was younger due to my natural proclivities. I am unabashedly extroverted and like to have fun and make genuine connections, and I've certainly never been known as the "quiet one". And all these tendencies made me into what was called a "natural leader". All through school and university, I held positions of leadership. Further, I was surrounded by a supportive lot – "Be yourself", my teachers and parents urged. "Your unique style is your biggest strength". And I naturally thought this would work well for me. Boy, was I in for a surprise.

As I progressed up the ranks and became a mid-level manager, my natural style became my enemy. True story (brace for impact) – Here are some of the things I heard as feedback: "You laugh too much", "Your voice is too loud", "People won't take you seriously or respect you because your dress is too colourful", and the pièce de resistance, "You need to be tougher if you want to succeed, you can't be so empathetic to your juniors".

Suffice it to say; I was in shock. The rules of the game I needed to abide by had changed under my nose. While the thought of not being myself was jarring, I was determined to succeed. And at that point, I didn't know better, so I changed myself. I decided to become much more like my male colleagues. Stamp down on my femininity, stamp down on any desire for work-life balance, be hyper-focused, and not tolerate "weaknesses". And never, ever, be vulnerable.

To some extent, I found success, but it felt hollow. Even worse, I hit a glass ceiling. You know, it's called a glass ceiling because it is not visible; you only realise it is there when you hit it.

The tragedy is that when women are confident – they are labelled cocky. When they are assertive, they are labelled aggressive. They are labelled ungrateful when they negotiate for more money to do more work. And when they are focused and driven, they are labelled "*ambitchious*".

To add insult to injury, even being "allowed" to run the race is considered a privilege. Women need to prove themselves more for the value they will bring. Women are often not considered a safe choice for leadership positions because they seem too different from the other leaders. People in power find the predictability and sameness of choosing someone from their gender, background, and social class reassuring.

Once I hit the glass ceiling, I had one of those life-changing moments. I had tried being "one of the blokes", and it got me thus far but no further. Now, I was faced with a choice – do I continue to struggle, not being true to myself, yet not succeeding? Or should I stand firm in my power, dare to be myself, and be the change I wanted to see in the world?

Luckily for me, around the same time I was at this crossroad, the world around us was waking up to the concept of diversity, equity and inclusion. Slowly but surely, "Authenticity", "Empathetic leadership", and "Equitable workplaces" became not just buzzwords but actual paradigm shifts that organisations embraced.

I was presented with an opportunity to join a much more inclusive workplace. Even though, from an external perspective, it might have seemed like a career step down for me, the fact that my values aligned with that of the company I joined meant that I was much happier. I could be my authentic self, and I was not penalised. In fact, my unique perspective was valued, and I progressed in my career by leaps and bounds.

By finding a playing field that allowed me to play to my strengths, I was able to succeed. And succeed not just in terms of career but also in terms of living a whole life – having a family, being able to pursue hobbies, travelling and having leisure time and, most importantly – to keep learning.

Today, I am very privileged to be in a senior role in a multinational corporation. I am in a position where I can make a difference in creating a more equitable workplace – by giving opportunities to deserving candidates, ensuring we have pay equity, by instating policies that can support women to lead a whole life and not have to choose between having a family and having financial freedom.

As millennials enter the workforce, the world is evolving around us. The terrain that the rabbit and turtle first ran in has changed. It is no longer just a playing field. Now it has become a jungle – which still has the terra-firma, but also has water bodies – and to navigate that, a diverse skill set is required.

With the changed context, having diversity is not just a "nice to have". Organisations have woken up to the diversity premium. Research[3] shows that diverse teams perform better than homogenous ones.

---

[3]Dixon-Fyle, Sundiatu et al. (May 19, 2020). *How Diversity, Equity and Inclusion Matter.* McKinsey & Company. https://www.mckinsey.com/featured-insights/diversity-and-inclusion/diversity-wins-how-inclusion-matters (accessed January 30, 2023).

But surface-level diversity is not enough – where one might look and sound different but is expected to think and behave exactly like the majority. The real benefits of diversity can only be unlocked by letting people bring their unique strengths to work. By creating a work environment where diversity can thrive – and people are paid equitably while also having a meaningful life outside work.

So if, by economic theory, it makes sense to reward diversity, why does the equity gap persist? This is where we need to look at how power is wielded. In a world run by rabbits, the rabbit will always be valued higher. So, for the value system to change, we would need more turtles to rise to power and create a reward system that equitably values the ability to navigate different terrains.

And that, for me, is what "Embracing Equity" is all about. It is not just about levelling the playing field; it is about redesigning the terrain to leverage the unique strengths of diversity and the economic value attached to it. To make it possible for people during different stages of life to be still running their race.

2023 is the year of the rabbit in the Lunar calendar. I would submit that it has been the era of the rabbit for a while. The time for change, for embracing equity, has come. Let's create a world where the turtles Don't have to be like rabbits to win. They can run their own race and find success – in every sense of the word.

ABOUT THE AUTHOR

Priyadarshini Sharma

Priyadarshini Sharma is a C-Suite corporate leader with over 23 years of multi-country, multi-industry experience in global blue-chip organisations. She has personally experienced several rites of passage. These include juggling career and motherhood, dealing with discrimination, and breaking through glass ceilings.

Armed with that experience, Priyadarshini became an author, a professional speaker, and a mentor to share her learning and inspire others to forge their own paths to greatness.

Originally from India, Priyadarshini has lived and worked in six countries, speaks five languages – including Mandarin, and calls Singapore home. A lifelong learner, she holds an MBA from the Indian Institute of Management, is an ICA-certified coach and is currently pursuing a degree certification in advanced business communications at Harvard.

Being an avid advocate for diversity, equity, and inclusion, Priyadarshini is committed to driving meaningful dialogue on issues of DEI and creating a more equitable and inclusive workplace.

You can connect with Priyadarshini at:

Speaker profile on KeyNoteWomen.com:
https://keynotewomen.com/speaker/priyadarshini-sharma

in : https://www.linkedin.com/in/priyadarshini-sharmasg/

STORY TWO

She Has No Presence

Was there a subject called "Presence" at university?

"She can't lead because she is too soft-spoken".

"She does not have the potential because she seldom speaks in meetings".

"She is too quiet. She is not smart enough".

"She has no presence!"

This is the feedback I was given when I first started working in the corporate world.

Presence? Was there a subject called "Presence" at university?

"Presence" was a foreign subject to me. When I was young, no one told me about being present. If anything, I was constantly taught not to be present. My mother's voice is still in my head, telling me, "The louder you are, the more trouble you will get into".

As I entered the corporate world, these voices, except that of my most loving mother, became more and more conflicting.

"You need to show your executive presence," one of my bosses, who had quite an alpha character, often told me. He saw me struggle to speak in meetings, especially when senior leaders were attending.

I grew up in a traditional Hong Kong Chinese family. Similar to many traditional families, sons are preferred over daughters. In traditional Chinese culture, the "son preference" is related mainly to agricultural economies, where males usually earn more than females due to their physical strength. They often thought once the girl was married, she would belong to the husband's family. They also believed that only sons could take care of the families. The male sides inherit the bloodlines of the families.

As I grew up, I gradually understood why my father thought so highly about sons. My father went through challenging times. He grew up as an orphan. Since he was young, he had to look after himself and his siblings. He started working and paying all the bills for the family when he was still a kid. He was often bullied and laughed at. As my father started his family, he inevitably emphasised the importance of stability, especially financial stability. To my father, the primary objective of getting married was to perpetuate his bloodline. Therefore he must have a son.

After giving birth to my elder sister, my mother wished and prayed that the second baby would be a boy. To the whole family's disappointment, I was born. For health reasons, my mother could not have more children. My relatives often comforted my parents with, "Never mind, as long as your girls learn to cook well and serve others well, they will marry rich guys. They will still be useful when they grow up".

Since I was young, I have always felt I was born inferior because I am a girl.

My father had a hot temper. To avoid triggering my father, my mother taught us how to behave, "Don't take up too much space. Just nod and obey. Don't speak in front of men. Always respect your elders. When they speak, just nod and obey".

I was clever at school. I often scored the highest in examinations. Teachers gave me various award certificates, from "best conduct" to "best in class". But I just wanted recognition from my father.

"These are just pieces of paper. Why are you so happy?" my father would ask. He did not see value in award certificates.

From a young age, I learnt not to cry because crying was considered a girl's behaviour. I still remember I was nine years old when the accident happened. My left thigh was severely burnt. The pain was excruciating. I can still recall the feeling of fire constantly burning the nerves inside my body. The blisters were all over my thighs. I was sent to the emergency ward. The nurses were surprised and said, "Little girl, you are so brave. How could you not cry?" The truth was, I was afraid. I was so scared that the moment my father saw me cry, he would think girls were useless, and I would be the useless girl again.

Psychologically, I felt neglected. As I grew up, I realised I was not alone. Research shows that 35% of women worldwide have experienced psychological or physical neglect at some point in their lives[4,5]. 47% of employees say that the voices of underrepresented people in their workplace are not

---

[4]World Health Organisation. (March 9, 2021). *Violence against Women.* World Health Organization. https://www.who.int/news-room/fact-sheets/detail/violence-against-women (accessed February 9 ,2023).

[5]United Nations Department of Economic and Social Affairs. (2015). *The World's Women 2015, Trends and Statistics.* United Nations. https://unstats.un.org/unsd/gender/downloads/worldswomen2015_report.pdf (accessed February 9, 2023).

represented[6]. Employees of colour especially feel that their voices are not heard no matter how hard they work. They become the invisible figures of the organisation.

Imagine working in a place where your voice is not heard. How could you possibly thrive?

To embrace equity, we must address the "rights in the air". Yes, the shared "air space" where Everyone's voice is worthy of being heard if one chooses to speak; the equity that protects Everyone's right to be heard. Don't get me wrong. I am not demanding equality whereby everyone says the same amount. I believe Everyone's natural conversational styles should be honoured. More introverted individuals may express themselves in other ways, not necessarily verbally. More extroverted individuals may speak their minds when they choose to. In the workplace, we should protect Everyone's right to be heard. It is not about frequency; it is about "presence".

I embarked on my journey of finding my presence. The change journey started over a decade ago when I switched careers from an entrepreneur to an investment banker. I realised whatever made me successful as an entrepreneur would not make me successful in the corporate world. The winning formula is different. Yes, you still have to work hard and work smart. But when you work in the corporate world, you must know how to carry yourself.

---

[6]WorkForce Institute. (2021). *The Heard and the Heard-Nots.* UKG workforceinstitute.org/wp-content/The-Heard-and-the-Heard-Nots (accessed February 9, 2023).

To progress in the new world, I needed to change. I needed to take up equity in the air space. I had to speak up.

After my MBA, I started my first corporate job in an investment bank in Hong Kong. All the managers and bosses were male. All of them were much more senior than me. My mother's voice came out again, " Don't speak in front of men. Always nod and obey the elders. When they speak, just nod and listen".

Other than "Hi" or "Good morning", I did not speak in most meetings. I sat in the corner of the meeting rooms. I kept my head down, jotting notes that I never really needed. I was not heard. I was not visible. Gradually people started ignoring me to the extent that they did not even include me in their meetings. That feeling was very familiar. The feeling of being neglected was exactly like how I felt when I was a little girl.

Hierarchical power became one of my greatest challenges at work. The power that I associated with all men and all seniors possessed. I gave away my power to others, simply because they were men or more senior to me. I gave away my power by not embracing the equity to speak.

The appraisal by my first boss hit me hard, "You have a good academic background. That's why I hired you. How could you be so dumb? Don't you even know how to speak?"

Dumb? Did he just call me dumb? I held my tears until I was home. I was helpless. I didn't know how to remove my mother's voice. I knew if I wanted to progress in professional settings, I must not give away any power. I must learn to speak up. As I was wiping tears, I saw a post-it notepad next to the tissue box. I took one post-it note and wrote "SPEAK UP" with my red marker pen. I posted this note on my laptop. I brought the note with me everywhere I worked.

I moved to Canada for my next chapter. The naïve me at that time thought things would improve automatically once I moved to a new work environment. "I have new colleagues. They Don't know me at all. There won't be any prejudice against me. I just need to dress up a bit to look professional".

The first day I arrived at the office, it was even worse. 95% of my colleagues were white males. Everyone spoke fluent English. There were a few Asian-looking colleagues. But the moment they spoke, you knew they were the bananas – yellow on the outside, white on the inside. They didn't know much about Asian culture. I was the only true-blue Asian Chinese. I wanted to blend in. I tried to mask my accent. As much as I listened to local radio or watched English TV channels 24/7, I could not de-accent my English.

All these white male colleagues carried themselves naturally. I felt their energy, power and confidence in the air when they walked past. I felt intimidated because they were male. As soon as I realised I was about to give away my power, my "SPEAK UP" note prompted me to behave differently.

What is the worst thing that could happen if I speak up? Other than being judged, nothing worse could happen. I worked extra hard every day to prepare for every meeting. I ensured I had my comments and questions structured in my mind in advance. I committed to speaking at least once in each meeting.

In the beginning, I was terrified. My heart pumped very fast. I was practising the sentences in my mind. I didn't listen to others. I was not present. "Oh, not present again?" I could not afford another lack of presence appraisal. I looked at my "SPEAK UP" note. I felt the need to speak. I did not jot notes at all this time. I forced myself to look into people's eyes and listened to what people had to say. I embraced the presence. I spoke.

"Hey! your grammar is wrong".

"You should have used past tense".

"It's plural. You forgot the 's'".

While I was bombarding myself with all these grammatical rules (by the way, I am sure my secondary school English teacher must be happy now that I remember all her grammar teaching), the most senior leader said, "What an innovative idea! Why have we not thought of it before?"

All of a sudden, I became the "ideas girl". People were keen to hear what ideas I had. They appreciated the new perspectives I brought. Being different was recognised as a strength by the team. People were more used to me speaking, to the extent that they would turn to me and wait for me to talk if I hadn't shared anything during the meetings. That was the most incredible relief I had ever experienced. Finally, my voice was welcomed. Finally, I felt my voice was worthy of being heard.

The dedication and courage to voice my views helped me advance my career. I was quickly promoted to a senior position in the finance department.

"No one knows you Don't have a technical background in finance. Conceal it. Don't show it. Just be curious and ask questions. You will pick things up along the way". I brainwashed myself that I was the right boss for the team on my way to meet them for the first time in person.

My direct reports were seated and waiting. The elephant in the room was, "Why are you being promoted?" I pretended I felt nothing.

I was nervous. I didn't know what to do. I swept their feelings under the carpet. I pretended to be confident and boasted about my achievements. I failed my first impression.

The next day, the team was supposed to sit with me and provide the lowdown on the business. The most experienced member started. After five minutes of technical jargon bombardments, I was utterly lost. I asked a few clarifying questions. The team gave a bunch of unhelpful answers, with a look insinuating, "You are such an idiot. What makes you our boss?" Frankly speaking, I was not offended. I empathised with them.

While I tried to avoid their eye contact, I saw the "SPEAK UP" note on my laptop. Yes, why was I not speaking my mind now? I figured the situation was so bad that nothing could get worse.

I turned off my laptop abruptly. And I started sharing what I felt and how I empathised with them. I acknowledged I did not have the technical expertise, but I had an open mind. I was committed to making this the best team so everyone could contribute in their way. I told them, "We all will thrive as long as we lean in".

To my surprise, the honesty and transparency melted the walls they had built against me. Since then, we have had a fantastic time working and constructively challenging each other.

Here you go. To embrace the equity that allows me to be heard was never about pretending to be someone I was not. I've learnt, it's about being honest and courageous enough to admit who you truly are, including in areas where you may seem inadequate. The more honest and brave you are with the people around you, the more likely they will accept your uniqueness. The moment you establish who you truly are and connect with others in your true self, the more likely others will respect you as an individual, not your title or your rank. And that state is where your sacred garden is – the space where you embrace your equity and get your authentic voice heard.

Have faith in protecting your space. Enjoy being who you truly are. You will be pleasantly surprised by how your world will evolve as you save your sacred gardens.

A few years ago, I had my first child. When the obstetrician revealed it was a girl, I was afraid to tell my father. After many sleepless nights, I finally called him, “Papa, I am pregnant. You are going to meet your first granddaughter soon”.

With tears in his eyes, my dad said, “As long as she is like you, I will be so proud”.

ABOUT THE AUTHOR

ADELE HUNG

Adele Hung is a global commercial director in one of the largest biopharmaceutical companies. She is an international keynote speaker based in Singapore. Her professional journey includes founding a healthcare consultancy in China's Greater Bay Area and working in investment banking. Adele has forged a successful career holding key leadership positions across marketing, digital and strategy functions.

Having lived and worked in the United Kingdom, Canada, Hong Kong, China and Singapore, Adele believes in cultural authenticity. She regularly speaks about diversity, equity, and inclusion in the workplace. Adele inspires people to overcome self-limiting beliefs by relating her transformational leadership stories and cultural experiences. In 2017 she established the Women Leadership Initiative in Singapore to support diversity and encourage active allyship in the workplace.

Adele holds a BSc in Speech Pathology and Behavioural Psychology and an MBA with Strategy and Finance majors.

She lives with her husband and their two young daughters.

You can connect with Adele at:

Speaker profile on KeyNoteWomen.com:
https://keynotewomen.com/speaker/adele-hung

✉ : hung.adele@gmail.com

in : https://www.linkedin.com/in/adele-hung/

STORY THREE

The System is Unfair, but You can Still Win

Equity in an ideal world.

When I was 11 years old, my family emigrated from the country I grew up in – Saudi Arabia. Despite its conservative reputation, life there was a fairytale.

I lived in a perfect world.

I had my mum and my dad.

We lived in a gated community, where all the houses looked the same.

Everyone had a garden. We shared a pool and played in a big sandpit (I loved that sandpit!). Life was a utopia.

Apparently not.

Back then, if you were a foreigner and wanted to set up a business, you needed a local business partner, who would have a 51% stake in the company. Call it the benefit of being a local, or the price of being a foreigner. It's all a matter of perspective.

So regardless of their contribution, the local partner (the one with the bigger share), would get more profit. My dad set up a company this way, but his local partner kept wanting more profits for no work.

That was a deal-breaker for my dad. So he decided to leave.

I didn't want to leave the place I grew up in, my school, my friends, and my beloved sandpit. Cartoons and books made me believe in happy endings. They taught me that the good guys always win. And as long as you were the "good guy" and followed the rules, you would win.

Moving to my father's birthplace – Egypt – was a cultural shock. Before the move, I remember my mother saying to me, "Yasmine, you have to be careful. Cairo is a dangerous place".

For an 11-year-old, who had lived in a fairy tale and had little experience with "danger," these comments were pretty jarring. And when we arrived in Cairo, I realised that the fairy tale didn't exist.

My mother's words started to feel real.

So why did this city feel unsafe?

Cairo is a city of over 20 million people. At that time, there were no gated communities and we were surrounded by hunger and poverty.

The first thing I noticed was the disparity. Every time we stopped at a traffic light I was confronted. Me with my clean clothes seated in an air-conditioned car, while kids just outside in rags, with stains on their faces, knocking on the window, begging for money.

I remember asking my dad, "papa, why aren't they in school?" He was visibly uncomfortable about having this conversation with me. After a long pause, he said, "Unfortunately, these children and their families are not privileged like us. To them education is a luxury they cannot afford".

Today I realise that it is impossible to understand and embrace equity without acknowledging this universal truth: Not everyone has the same privilege.

The World Has Never Been Fair

Children, by nature, want the world to be good and fair. So even with the knowledge that I was more fortunate than many. I still didn't understand why everyone couldn't have everything…or at least the same as me.

Food, healthcare, education, resources. How come some have a surplus of things, while others barely have anything?

It's undoubtedly unfair. But here's the hard pill to swallow: fighting for the world to be absolutely fair is a losing battle.

My "international" education allowed me opportunities for growth and exposure that those kids outside the car didn't have. Unfair.

My dad was being pressured into giving away 51% of what he worked for, just because he didn't have the "right passport". Unfair.

My household and society ingrained in me that my gender would always be at a disadvantage. Unfair.

As a heterosexual woman, I've never had to deal with people ostracising me because of my gender and partner choice. That is such a contrast from the millions who are denied opportunities, representation and fair treatment simply because of their same-sex and non-gendered partners. Unfair.

As unfortunate as it is, the world has different starting points for different people. Most people Don't get a kickstart. Some have more resources than others; some, more connections. But for a lot of people, like those kids at the traffic lights, the unfairness is a lot more critical; it is about survival.

But I will say this: I Don't think it is all our fault. While we perpetuate it, a good part of it is generational; some of it is a trauma response. Our ancestors struggled with colonialism, wars, famine, illiteracy and what-not.

So what can we do?

That's what I am going to show you in this chapter. So that you can learn how to develop patterns to play in an unfair system, and use it to your advantage.

Despite being antagonised by peers and bosses about my age, race, experience, and learning disability. Using these tools helped, because I challenged the unspoken narrative.

Embracing equity in an unfair world can be a challenging task, but all hope is not lost.

How do we Embrace Equity?

There are several ways to work towards creating a more equitable society.

On the hygiene level, yes we can...

1. Educate ourselves and others about the systemic issues that lead to inequality.
2. Creating inclusive environments, policies and procedures in your workplace, school, or community.
3. Holding people and institutions accountable for their actions and policies that perpetuate inequality.

It is important to remember that equity is not about treating everyone the same. But rather acknowledging and addressing the unique barriers and challenges that the marginalised groups face, and taking steps to level the playing field.

But we have heard that already…

We can't embrace equity by telling people to "speak up," or "beat the system". Doing that is easier said than done. Many people are not even aware they can play the game.

For instance, once, when I was 11, I found myself in the school field, getting briefed about a friendly softball match. Surrounded by kids – most of whom were strangers – from all grades. It was intimidating.

When the coach split us up into groups, one of the boys pointed towards us,

"They can't play".

"Why not?"

"They are girls".

Silence.

The coach said nothing, and neither did we.

Someone finally spoke the unspoken narrative. An invisible story that we Don't see, but is understood. This felt uncomfortable. Some girls decided they didn't want to play anymore. And our small group became smaller.

That was the first time I had heard that I was not good because of my sex.

As the coach went over the instructions, I went through a storm of emotions. I was angry and frustrated. What does me wanting to play a game have to do with me being a girl? I didn't like being boxed in because of my gender.

It was unfair. I was annoyed at the girls who abandoned the game, and myself for not being able to articulate my frustration.

I was so lost in sorting out my feelings that I barely heard the instructions. When the game started, I looked the boy directly in the eye, as if to say, "I can play, and I have every right to be here".

I walked up, ready to bat, and looked around the field. All the players were in position… waiting to dismiss me. I got in position as the pitcher threw the ball.

He swung his arm, and aimed the ball right at me.

I saw it coming towards me, and swung the bat.

I missed it.

The boy – the very same – laughed triumphantly. "See, I told you girls can't play". Others chimed in. And the humiliation I felt at the time infuriated me even more.

"I will show you that I can play," I repeatedly chanted to myself.

As the pitcher pitched the ball, I swung the bat with all my might – channelling all my anger into that one swing. I heard a sound, but it took me a second to realise that my bat had made contact with the ball.

“Run!” my best friend yelled from the game.

Even though the ball went far enough to ensure I would get to the base, I still ran like my life depended on it. I felt vindicated. I turned to the boy and said, “I thought you said girls can’t play”.

I didn’t care how the rest of the game panned out. A homerun. I proved my point.

That day, I learnt an important lesson; the world will test you and it’s up to you whether you choose to play, or get played. The hard truth is that not all games will be fair. In some games, you’ll be at a clear advantage. In others, not so much.

I decided to change the narrative. I insisted on playing, I had a chance of starting a new narrative. That day most of the girls left before even playing. They never stood a chance because they believed the unspoken narrative.

A lot of people Don’t even know that they have the option to play the game, let alone speak up against it or contribute to change.

So, when we find ourselves playing in an unfair system; a system that is rigged against us because of our class, gender, race, nationality, sexual preference or age; how do we play and change the system?

I know this sounds great in theory, and impossible to execute but the fact is that there have been many great game-changers. Heard of Rosa Parks, Jacinda Arden, Trevor Noah,

Maya Angelou, Greta Thunberg, Chelsea Manning, Nawal El Saadawi who were disadvantaged whether because of their gender, race, age or resources, but who still managed to tap into their potential and unlock their power.

They choose to challenge and contribute to the narrative. They become unforgettable authorities whose new perspective made a world of difference.

Systemic barriers can limit the success of marginalised groups, but there are ways to work towards achieving that success despite these challenges.

- **Building a support system:** Surround yourself with people who will challenge you. Sometimes our family, friends, mentors, and community members will maintain the unspoken narrative. If you Don't have that support system, network until you do.
- **Seeking out resources:** There are books, podcasts, mentors, coaches, programmes that can help you. If you can't afford it, there are scholarships, and grants that provide financial assistance. I got scholarships for both my undergrad and masters or else I couldn't have afforded it. Some people are embarrassed, but we all have different starting points.
- **Developing resilience:** Learn how to cope with the stress and disappointment that can come with facing systemic barriers.
- **Being proactive:** Take the initiative to create opportunities for yourself, such as starting your

own business, applying for internships or jobs, and networking with people in your field. The internet has meant you can build a brand and make money with lower barriers than ever before.

It's important to remember that success is not a one-size-fits-all concept. Everyone's definition of success may vary. Therefore, it's important to define your own goals and aspirations and focus on one battle at a time.

Slowly, society starts to give us more examples of this newfound wisdom.

Embracing Equity Starts Inside

Today, when I say, "I am a woman", I know I am strong. I have stopped giving my power away and being a victim of circumstance.

I now embrace being a woman; I own it and create a definition in a way that makes sense in the world I want to see.

To arrive at this, I had to understand and embrace that we need to move from old perspectives, and to change beliefs. I just asked myself the question, "what am I good at?"

Once I embraced this idea and began to live by it, I felt good at how I was starting to do things. I began to ask myself the questions, "What if I could be the victor in my own story?" "What if you can help transform the next generation to see what's possible for them too?"

You ought to ask yourself these questions too. Why not choose a story that you and I would be proud to leave as a legacy? That deep work sometimes takes us to question our identity and our beliefs. Of course, this takes us to the next phase.

We Need to Understand Our Gap

Part of knowing how to play the system is understanding how everyone fits in, how to leave the unspoken narratives in your head and to understand the people you are playing with and what they care about.

I learnt this the hard way. And it was hard, because when I was learning this I had never done it before. I didn't know how much I didn't know.

It was my pride to refuse to learn and leverage the experience of people who had tried before me. People who could teach me how to shortcut the process. My unspoken narrative was that "If I didn't know it myself, I was not good enough".

But the reality was I would never be good enough if I kept doing the same thing without learning what I was doing wrong.

Whenever I work with a leader or team who embraces equity, I start with learning what they truly want and teach them how to voice it into the world without being apologetic. It's also about developing their skills to sell their ideas and put them into the world.

For example, one of my coaching clients, a brilliant leader, whose leadership and initiatives helped her save her company half a billion dollars.

Yet – she did not know how to own her wins. Instead, she labelled herself as "I am a behind the scenes leader". Her labelling and her inability to communicate her achievements, held her back.

What about you, are you able to articulate your achievements? Or are you needing to develop this skill? If you are unable, are you taking the time to dive deeper and have a better understanding? Because if you don't, people will assume things and use their mental shortcuts to put you in a box. Failing to articulate your achievements is NOT a way to break the cycle; it is NOT a way to embrace equity.

We will not have equity when we choose to wait for things to be fair; it won't be fair. It will never be fair for a child to not have access to food. It will never be fair for a couple in love to be denied being together. It will never be fair that a leader won't get promoted because of the colour of their skin or the accent of their voice.

If we Don't let go and we Don't learn the skills to play in the system. We never get to change the world.

Your Decisions, Your Choices

Embracing equity is both an inner and an outer journey. You can only arrive at the destination if you move with the awareness that the conditions will never be perfect.

Once we fully acknowledge this imperfection, we can move forward, dive deeper, and understand some of the limiting narratives that have been passed down to us, and subsequently break the cycles in our own world.

We must adapt to acquire the skills needed to play this system. That is the only way we can become more assertive and make progressive changes to the system, instead of waiting for permission.

We need to think beyond ourselves and start thinking about what we can do to use the unfair system and create something fair for the world. That kind of power is not only contagious, but also transformative. Creating new, better, fairer systems is the only way to restore equity in the world.

ABOUT THE AUTHOR

YASMINE KHATER

Yasmine Khater enables leaders to connect, stand out, and sell their ideas with ease. All while inspiring their team, attracting more clients, and growing their business (and careers).

She is the lead researcher and Head Story Coach at the Sales Story Method. Her company's mission is to help leaders fall in love with sales and become persuasive storytellers.

Armed with a degree in psychology and communications. She is an aspiring "armchair" neuroscientist who loves to study how to improve sales by applying science to the brain.

For the past decade, Yasmine has helped thousands of leaders from companies like Salesforce, Agilent, Essilor, LinkedIn, Credit Suisse and more.

She comes from a mixed heritage, has lived in seven countries, and she's travelled to a quarter of the world. In her free time, Yasmine is an adventurer, from trips to the Arctic to cycling through some of the world's toughest mountain terrains. She is also a game developer under the brand letslearntoconnect.com.

You can connect with Yasmine at:

Speaker profile on KeyNoteWomen.com:
https://keynotewomen.com/speaker/yasmine-khater

: http://www.salesstorymethod.com/

: https://www.linkedin.com/in/thesalesstoryteller/

STORY FOUR

The Power of Intentional Listening

Science is showing the powerful role listening plays in business outcomes.

I expected a smooth transition when I moved to Germany at 30. I couldn't speak German but was confident I could immerse myself, study hard and be fluent within three months. I was ready to connect with people and have influence in the same way I did at home. I was excited and had no fear of the journey ahead.

Shortly after I arrived, a lady came to my new apartment to help sew curtains for the windows. I kept looking at my husband as she spoke so he could translate. Later, she whispered to my sister-in-law, "Why does your brother have to permit his wife to make a decision?" She had assumed my non-verbal communication represented passive behaviour and a controlling husband. Little did she know my personality was the complete opposite. She listened in one way and misunderstood the context and my behaviours.

Three months later, I was homesick for the first time. I was experiencing culture shock and was in a deep hole. I used to be independent. Now I needed help to get things done. I used to be a well-respected business owner in my community, and people knew my name. Overnight, I felt labelled as "an American wife who should teach English".

I was unable to jump into conversations easily or was unintentionally left out. I missed taking part in those subtle jokes. I kept breaking informal rules; even strangers would confront me and tell me about my mistakes. Since I didn't understand the language well, helpful people were planning my life for me and forgetting to ask for my input or inform me. I was much quieter and more exhausted by intensely trying to keep up.

I was still unaware of the significant role listening would play on my journey as a woman, how I listened to myself, how others listened to me and how decisions were made based on the effectiveness of the listening in the moment.

Fast forward 20 years. My understanding of listening has expanded. And how different ways of listening or not listening shape the world around us.

Let's consider a few examples. Listening to understand. Listening to evaluate. Listening to values. Listening to cultural differences. Listening beyond our assumptions. Listening out of fear. Listening for solutions. Listening to silence. Listening with curiosity. Listening with judgement. Listening deeply to connect life and business decisions. Listening with presence. And the list goes on.

Intentionally choosing how to listen has consequences, and becoming aware of our natural patterns of listening and then intentionally choosing to listen differently has a powerful impact on the next steps we take and how we impact each other. I have learnt that embracing equity requires embracing intentional listening.

Embracing intentional listening involves actively trying to understand individuals' and groups' thoughts, feelings, and experiences while using that understanding to empower and support them. When we intentionally listen and respond to what we listen to with care, we listen much differently than the average listener. It involves non judgment, empathy, validation, and a desire for mutual understanding.

Dr Avi Kluger and Dr Guy Itzchakov published the results of their meta-data analysis on the power of listening at work. They concluded that listening generates high-quality connections that improve organisational outcomes, including greater creativity, productivity, clarity, and well-being for the listener, the speaker, and the organisation[7].

Imagine a world if we intentionally listened to embrace women's equity in the workforce and how this would ultimately hugely impact successful business outcomes.

We have moments where we listen well and moments where we listen terribly, if at all. Listening is often impacted by who we listen to, how we listen, when, and how often we listen.

After learning basic German, it was time to find a job. The weekend before, I went to a party in Hanover. I began speaking with a helpful woman who was ready to advise me on finding a job. "You have to get an internship first," she said. I was confused. I had already worked ten years in academia and even owned my own business for seven years.

I left the party with the conversation out of my mind. On Monday morning, though, I saw an English-speaking position for an internship in a corporate communications

---

[7]Kluger, A.N. and Itzchakov, G. (October 26, 2021) "The Power of Listening at Work". *Annual Reviews.* https://www.annualreviews.org/doi/abs/10.1146/annurev-orgpsych-012420-091013 (accessed February 12, 2023).

department at a global company nearby. I applied. On Wednesday, my telephone rang. My interview was scheduled for Friday. My new boss promised me that even though they couldn't give me a job then, she would give me a great experience. I accepted the opportunity.

This door opened because my boss and I were listening to opportunities and the value we could bring each other. I could practice my German and experience a new work environment without pressure. She was excited about bringing in a new perspective and leveraging my English.

Within one and half years, I started as an intern and was promoted to a senior manager role. Even though I worked very hard, without my boss listening to me, opening doors, protecting me and ensuring that I had what I needed to develop, I would never have made it on my own.

I was asked to set up best practices and measurements for our department during my internship. Within a few weeks, I researched the most up-to-date data and reached out to my network, setting up calls with the heads of communications so that we could share best practices. In our one-on-one meeting, I showed her my results, and she looked at me with big eyes asking, "I have been trying to get something done for years. How did you get this done so quickly?"

This innocent question potentially came from multiple assumptions: First, an intern is inexperienced and cannot produce senior work. Second, if my senior team didn't manage, how can an intern be so efficient?

At that moment, I realised I was in an "intern" box. In reality, I was an intern only in title. Even at 30 years old, I had already taught at university, owned my own business and lived in multiple cultures. The goal was not hard. What was needed was interest and focused time.

Since my strength is to listen and network, I was able to connect with experts and facilitate conversations where current practices could be shared authentically. As my boss listened to me, her assumptions dropped away. She began to see me with a renewed perspective, shifting my journey within the organisation.

She realised that even though I may not have the same experience as her current team, I brought other strengths beyond my English and my degrees. I was flexible and calm. I was good at building relationships. I loved learning and growing. I was strategic and created more visibility for our team.

Over time, my awareness of having limitations as a woman minority with a language barrier increased. Understanding how intentional listening plays a powerful role towards creating inclusive and strategic leadership became more apparent, as did the impact it has had on my productivity and my well-being. I experienced how incredible leaders are also human. And I experienced my own humanness. Only our willingness to listen and co-create an equitable environment together will help pioneer a path forward for successful business outcomes and incredible team cohesiveness.

In the beginning, I didn't know all the formal and informal rules of working in a different country. One day a male colleague burst into my office upset that I did not do a final approval with him before an article was published. Just the day before, we had a meeting to discuss changes. I followed through quickly, got the job done and sent it out.

In German-speaking meetings, I had to listen beyond the words. I paid attention to the context, the flow of conversation and who seemed to influence who. I noticed when eyes lit up and when minds checked out. I learnt to pay attention to details around me that could help give me clarity, even if I wasn't 100% clear about the words. I learnt to ask questions for deeper understanding. I learnt how to ask my peers for insight into the context.

I discovered that by being interested in the other person, the door to the relationship would open, and interest would be reciprocated. Sometimes not understanding opinions and assumptions allowed me to take unexpected next steps, surprising my colleagues with what was possible. Sometimes they were happy. Sometimes they were jealous. My goal was to listen calmly, pay attention to their deeper needs and fears and ultimately, stay professional no matter their reaction.

One time, I almost gave up.

In Germany, a woman can take maternity leave with income for ten months after her child's birth. This is incredible for women's equity. Most German women took the full time off.

Because of my American mindset, I asked for 15 hours of

work per week after two months, even if this meant the same income. I wanted to stay connected to my network, and honestly, I liked to work. Another woman was hired for one year to cover my maternity leave. As I share this story, I want to emphasise that a lot of what happened next was based on unconscious bias', unconscious individual fears, and lack of consideration of the consequences and impact on my reputation from everyone involved, even myself.

I was responsible for a "smaller", otherwise less important business area to "help" me manage my time as a new mother. Even though I went into the office once a week, I was often asked, "When are you coming back to work?" Even though I explained my work schedule, my answer still did not connect because it wasn't normal to work from home, especially during maternity leave. I realised I was in a predicament. My unique decision was not a part of the reality my colleagues had experienced before. Not only was my work not valued, but I also didn't even feel seen.

I didn't have the energy to fight. I decided to do my best and enjoy my flexibility in caring for my son.

Ten months later, I returned to work full-time. Still sleep-deprived and breastfeeding, I was looking forward to returning to the office. Everyone seemed to welcome me with open arms on the surface, but I realised very soon that there was a crack in my reputation. Rumours had started while I was gone, creating the impression that I couldn't perform well because I was not fluent in German. Also, the last big project I ran before going on maternity leave was given a prestigious communication award. For some reason, I was not informed, and because I was not in the office every day, I couldn't intervene. And no one intervened for me. The night of the celebration, I was not seen on stage with the team to receive the award and credit for my hard work.

I confronted my boss about the situation. Even though she is one of the best leaders I know, she is also human. And the intensity of the work environment, deadlines and incredible pressures didn't give her the space to see the whole picture. Yet, instead of defending or making excuses, she listened.

We paused and objectively looked at the situation. Just as I was honest with her, she was also honest and reflective with me. "Are you happy in this job because you are so different from this team? If you want to find another job, I will help you. If you want to stay on this team, I will support you in any way possible. But you need to know that I need someone to get the job done well. This can be you, and it can also be someone else".

After a good night's sleep, I informed her I wanted to stay on the team. At lightning speed, she scheduled meetings with all important stakeholders whose perceptions mattered. We evaluated the data and found that my output was solid, and German was not a barrier. After debunking this perception, we listened to our stakeholders and what was on their minds and hearts. We were listening for trust.

This allowed me to increase the quality of my work while also better managing my time as a working mother. And I developed even stronger stakeholder relationships which increased my reputation, which follows me to this day.

If my boss had not listened and supported me with multiple resources and her strong belief in my potential, my chances for success would have decreased incredibly. What I needed was different from what my team members needed to thrive. Equality is not equity.

We are just discovering how individuals and organisations can practice intentional listening and promote equity for women. Here are some steps that can be taken:

- Enjoy listening to your biases: Instead of judging or defending your biases, find simple and light ways to increase your awareness. Before going into a conversation, write down your assumptions about the other person, the situation, and the context. Listen with curiosity and interest at the meeting as if you are watching a movie for the first time. Check these assumptions afterwards and be willing to change.
- Have an intentional listening team: Ask 3-5 different people to listen to you with intention regularly. High-quality listening helps us self-reflect, become more aware and change our perceptions[8].
- Be an intentional listener: Have you noticed how when someone listens to you well, you speak better? If you are authentically interested, she will speak more clearly and

---

[8]Itzchakov, G. (November 2020). "Can high quality listening predict lower speakers' prejudiced attitudes?" *Science Direct.* https://www.sciencedirect.com/science/article/pii/S0022103120303620 (accessed February 12, 2023).

with more charisma. This will help her find her voice in the organisation.

- Listen with your whole body: Be present and fully engaged in the conversation. This means putting aside mental and physical distractions. When you are aware of your whole body and emotions, the quality of your listening and what you understand beyond words will surprise you.
- Ask one open-ended question at a time and listen after[9]. Ask a question that starts with what and how. More information will be shared without getting quiet or defensive. And never ask a question if you are not ready to listen.
- Pause instead of interrupt: What if pausing were an opportunity to think clearly?[10] Don't interrupt. Listen with intention as someone speaks. A pause of silence may be a thoughtful reflection on what was just said to know what to say next. In meetings, having 1-2 minute

---

[9]Van Quaquebeke, N. (n.d.). "Leaders and Asking Questions: The Surprising Discovery of What Is Needed to Find Solutions and Build Relationships". *Listening Alchemy* (podcast), https://listeningalchemy.com/listen-in/leaders-and-asking-questions-the-surprising-discovery-of-what-is-needed-to-find-solutions-and-build-relationships-with-niels-van-quaquebeke/ (accessed February 12, 2023).

[10]Wolfe, J. and Powell, E. (2022). "Positive and Future-Focused vs. I-Focused: A Comparative Examination of Effective Conflict Resolution Scripts to Minimize Gender Backlash in Engineering Settings". Research Gate. https://www.researchgate.net/publication/360096972_Positive_and_Future-Focused_vs_I-Focused_A_Comparative_Examination_of_Effective_Conflict_Resolution_Scripts_to_Minimize_Gender_Backlash_in_Engineering_Settings (accessed February 12, 2023).

slots of silence for everyone to think before answering will encourage more meaningful answers, and everyone is more likely to listen to each other.

- Take meaningful action based on listening: When inequalities or discrimination are identified, act. This can include changing policies, processes and practices within the organisation or industry. Ask for suggested solutions.
- Grow your listening muscle: intentional listening requires regular practice to strengthen.

These are foundational steps for individuals and organisations to develop skills and promote more inclusive and equitable environments. Science is showing the powerful role listening plays in business outcomes. This underlines how intentional listening is required to embrace equity to work smarter and feel better together.

ABOUT THE AUTHOR

Raquel Ark

Raquel Ark, MA, CPC, is a podcast host, speaker, mentor, coach and trainer. She has

over 25 years of experience in multinational corporations and academia. She is the Founder of listening ALCHEMY, a communication training and coaching organisation including foundational, evidence-based listening programmes.

Her clients include HelloFresh, hotjar, commercetools, Codility, BASF, Fairtrade International and more. She is the podcast host of the listening SUPERPOWER podcast focused on listening in teams and organisations beyond what we typically consider.

Raquel has spoken on the TEDx stage, as well as at conventions, organisations and at schools both in person and remotely. She is the President of the International Listening Association and a university instructor at Fresenius University of Applied Sciences in Germany.

You can connect with Raquel at:

Speaker profile on KeyNoteWomen.com:
https://keynotewomen.com/speaker/raquel-ark

: https://www.linkedin.com/in/raquel-ark-b2067613/

: https://listeningalchemy.com/

STORY FIVE

Mind Your Language

The good news is that language is never fixed.

How often do you choose the words you use carefully or think about the meaning or subtext they might subliminally convey?

Probably not often unless you're in a situation like a job interview where you might pore over your words before you say them. Typically, we use language automatically and habitually; words, phrases and sayings are said without conscious analysis or thought about what they might be subtly reinforcing.

When I lived and worked in Singapore, I recall a short visit to the UK around the time Brexit happened. I had several conversations with people who'd voted for Brexit because of concerns about immigration (a particularly divisive topic at the time) about the difference between expats, immigrants, and foreign workers. While the differences are largely semantic, each is loaded with assumptions about wealth, education and social status. However, effectively, they all describe someone living and working in a country they're not native to.

Not having voted for Brexit myself, I deliberately provoked a reaction by describing myself as an economic migrant, which resulted in some interesting – and occasionally heated – conversations. "No, you're an expat!" But I was working in a foreign country. Surely "economic migrant" was just as appropriate a descriptor? Whether others agree is depended on how they felt about immigration. It got me thinking about how subtleties in language can reinforce our biases.

Language experts have long debated whether the language

we use is a mirror reflecting our culture back at us, or a way of shaping our beliefs and worldviews and influencing our behaviour. In my opinion, it has a significant role to play in both. It can perpetuate stereotypes and discrimination, reinforce gender norms, and make it difficult for individuals to break away from societal expectations.

So when we're aiming for gender equity, are the words we use holding women back?

Gender bias in language takes many forms. I studied English language and linguistics at college and university. Since then, during my more than 20 years career as a researcher, I've studied how people talk, what they say (and what they Don't) and how this links with their behaviour. And it's fascinating. People, when you start to observe and analyse their words and behaviour, are a multitude of contradictions.

We Don't always know why we behave or act in certain ways since much of our behaviour is habitual and driven by quick, intuitive reactions. In the same way, our language is driven by fast thinking, and we default to familiar words, phrases and sayings common to our specific culture or society. We might claim to be all for equity, but our words can subtly undermine our best intentions.

There are many obvious examples of gendered or sexist language common in everyday English. We're socialised to think of men as the default and women as the exception through the use of "he" in many situations rather than "she" or gender-neutral "they". Many professions are assumed to be "men"; Chairman, or Policeman, rather than neutral forms like "Chair" or "Police Officer". This is changing, albeit slowly, and these examples are rather more obvious than some of the subtler messages woven into the fabric of our language.

Language helps to brainwash us into specific gender roles at an early age. We reinforce girls from a young age, much more so than boys. We encourage them to dress up, wear makeup, look after their hair, and play quietly and nicely. Girls who Don't fit these conventions, rejecting a focus on appearance and dress, are told they're not very ladylike, not feminine or are labelled "tomboys".

By focusing on their exterior assets rather than their personality, we're grooming them to understand their worth and value are tied up with their appearance. By making sure they "play nicely", we're conditioning them into a gender stereotype of being passive and avoiding confrontation.

While toy stores might be making progress with gender-neutral toys, we still find examples in the language of boys' and girls' clothes reflecting and reinforcing traditional gender roles. In 2021, Sainsbury's in the UK sold t-shirts aimed at boys with the slogan "Let's go on a wild adventure" while the girls' equivalent said "Let's stay home". In 2022,[11] Primark was

---

[11]Whitehead, J. (October 13, 2021) "Sainsbury's children's clothing tells girls to 'stay home' and boys they're 'unstoppable'". *The Independent.* https://www.independent.co.uk/life-style/health-and-families/sainsburys-childrens-clothes-gender-stereotypes-b1937644.html (accessed February 10, 2023).

similarly called out[12], selling boys' tops with slogans such as "You are limitless" and "Fearless", while the equivalent girls' fare was emblazoned with "Keep on smiling" and "Be kind".

What are we doing if not subtly conditioning our young women from an early age to lack ambition or adventure and leave that to the men? What narratives are we subconsciously perpetuating, if not that boys are all about action and ambition, while girls are about feelings and emotions?

We criticise people who "run", "play", or "throw *like girls*", microaggressions against an entire gender, which write off half of the population as inferior and incapable of playing sports.

We condition girls into thinking they are genetically predisposed to doing less well than boys in academic areas which are typically male-dominated, such as maths or physics, so much so that they can perform badly through having fixed mindsets about these subjects[13]. We should praise their effort and willingness to learn rather than saying, "You're so good at [maths] for a girl". No wonder only 35% of STEM (Science, Technology, Engineering and Mathematics)

---

[12]"Primark accused of selling hugely sexist kids clothes". (February 7, 2022). *BBC News.* https://www.bbc.co.uk/news/business-60290232 (accessed February 10, 2023).

[13]Peak Wellbeing. (July 4, 2016). "The Truth About People Who Are Good At Math". *Medium.* https://medium.com/@peaklabs/the-truth-about-people-who-are-good-at-math-73dba22c31b7 (accessed February 3, 2023).

students in higher education globally are women[14] if we reinforce that they're the exception rather than the norm in specific academic fields.

That's why people may claim not to be sexist or misogynistic and then, in the next sentence, say something biased – often without recognising it. It's easily done because the language we use and gender biases we associate with specific words or phrases are so deeply entrenched in our culture, our communications and our way of thinking we Don't even notice them until we start to consciously become aware of the specific words we're using and their impact. As a scholar of English, and as I've become more aware of the subtle biases inherent in our speech, I've started to scrutinise my language much more – especially when interacting with my young nieces or other children.

This doesn't end in childhood, as these subtle narratives continue into adulthood. Society tells people to "man up", which, according to the *Oxford English Dictionary*[15] is to "demonstrate toughness or courage when faced with a difficult situation". Not only is the subtext that women can't

[14]UNESCO. (2022). "A Snapshot of Gender Inequality: 50 of The World's Most Sexist Laws, Policies & Norms". *United Nations Foundation.* https://equaleverywhere.org/app/uploads/2022/02/Equal-Everywhere-Snapshot.pdf. (accessed February 3, 2023).

[15]Yusuf, H. (June 24, 2019). "Is it OK to tell someone to 'man up'?" *BBC News.* https://www.bbc.co.uk/news/uk-48743113 (accessed February 10, 2023).

demonstrate toughness or resilience as well as men can, but it also suggests men who experience challenges and admit to having emotions are weak, unmanly, and by implication, less worthy males.

Gender narratives also follow us into the workplace. While male leaders are viewed positively for being "assertive", "decisive", and "direct", women in leadership positions are subject to a different standard of scrutiny and described as being "bossy" or "bitchy" for displaying the same characteristics[16]. These terms reinforce our judgements of women's competence, the notion that women lack qualities we typically associate with strong leaders and are more emotional and, therefore, less competent than men. They have serious ramifications in business; men are still significantly more likely to hold the majority of top leadership positions, and it's estimated that we're unlikely to reach global parity until somewhere between 2039 and 2070[17].

Women are infantilised through language, a subtle but additional way of portraying them as weak and subordinate. Grown men are unlikely to be referred to as 'boys', while women are frequently referred to as "girls". It's so embedded

---

[16]Agarwal, P. (October 23, 2018). "Not Very Likeable: Here Is How Bias Is Affecting Women Leaders". *Forbes.* https://www.forbes.com/sites/pragyaagarwaleurope/2018/10/23/not-very-likeable-here-is-how-bias-is-affecting-women-leaders/ (accessed February 10, 2023).

[17]Ghosh, I. (March 29, 2021). "The boardroom still has a gender gap: Here's what it looks like - and how to fix it". *World Economic Forum.* https://www.weforum.org/agenda/2021/03/study-shows-the-state-of-female-representation-on-corporate-boards/ (accessed February 10, 2023).

in English culture that women are a key user of "girls" in this context – "I'm going out with the girls" is as applicable to taking out one's young daughters as it is to going to a bar with a group of 40-odd-year old friends. While many wouldn't recognise this as a problem, it subconsciously infantilises women and subtly undermines their agency as adults – and importantly, there isn't a male equivalent.

We have double standards in language everywhere. Being an "eligible bachelor" is a positive, while the nearest female equivalent, "spinster", has pejorative associations and no male equivalent. Men who sleep around are "studs" or "stallions", images of strength and power, while women are "slags" or "sluts", shameful terms with dirty and negative associations.

But as well as biases in gendered language, we also have to be aware of our biases with language when it comes to how we think about and describe behaviours, actions, people etc., how this reflects our culture, and how it perpetuates stereotypes.

The number of derogatory synonyms for a woman's vagina compared to the male organ is astonishing. Of course, there are many alternative words for penis, but most are neutral or even positive – 'willy' or 'trouser-snake'. Many of the female equivalent terms are hardly neutral and, at worst, are animalistic ("beaver"), evoke butchery or violence ("gash" or "slit") or are otherwise deemed highly offensive in everyday conversation.

Some groups have attempted to reclaim keywords used negatively by society, such as the reclaiming of "queer" by

LGBTQIA+ communities, reflecting both a shift in language usage and society's views on sexuality and gender[18]. But reclaiming the word "cunt", even when Eve Ensler advocated it in her powerful 1997 *The Vagina Monologues*[19], which has since been performed thousands of times around the world, hasn't worked, and it remains one of the most offensive words in the English language even today.

And then there are the double standards of women dating younger men being labelled "cougars" while men dating younger women are…well, they're either just men, or they're the rather more glamourised "silver foxes".

Again, there's no female equivalent to a silver fox. Women are just old or over the hill. And, if they're famous and ageing, they're likely to disappear completely from our TV screens while men continue to act or present for many more years[20]. The lack of representation of older women on our screens is a cultural rather than language-specific issue. Still, terms like "silver foxes" with no female equivalent reflect this

---

[18]Clark, M. (February 9, 2021). "Queer' history: A history of Queer". *National Archives.* https://blog.nationalarchives.gov.uk/queer-history-a-history-of-queer/. (accessed February 10, 2023).

[19]Wikipedia, (December 22, 2022). "The Vagina Monologues". *Wikipedia.* https://en.wikipedia.org/wiki/The_Vagina_Monologues. (accessed February 3, 2023).

[20]Morgan, C. (November 26, 2019). "TV's gender AGE gap revealed: Male presenters are twice as likely to be employed past the age of 50 as women – with up to 22 YEARS difference between presenters on popular shows". *Mail Online.* https://www.dailymail.co.uk/femail/article-7723827/The-gender-age-gap-British-TV.html (accessed February 10, 2023).

element of our culture – and language and culture reinforce and perpetuate one another, so they are intrinsically linked.

The media are key agents in perpetuating stereotypes and using inflammatory language to drive sales, and they are very influential in day-to-day British culture. We're brainwashed into thinking it's okay to criticise women and hold them to a different standard than men because that's what we read about and it's "normal".

In 2023 the BBC – which claims to be fair and unbiased in its reporting – caused immediate outrage online for asking the question, "Can women really have it all?"[21] – subtext, "Can women really have the same as men?" – when Jacinda Ardern announced she was relinquishing her role as New Zealand's Prime Minister. That this question is still being asked shows how embedded in culture this phrase has become that even the BBC doesn't recognise it for what it is – sexist at best (no one asks the same question about men), misogynistic at worst.

Hatred and vitriolic content is regularly levelled at women in the media in a way it isn't with men. Take well-known TV presenter Jeremy Clarkson's recent comments about Meghan Markle where he "dreamt of the day when Meghan was 'made to parade naked through the streets of every town in

---

[21]TN Viral Desk. (January 21, 2023). "BBC apologises for 'sexist' Jacinda Ardern headline after social media backlash". *Times Now News.* https://www.timesnownews.com/viral/jacinda-ardern-resignation-headline-faces-backlash-for-being-sexist-as-bbc-apologises-article-97189162 (accessed February 10, 2023).

Britain while the crowds chant, "Shame!" and throw lumps of excrement at her"[22]. How is it acceptable to write that as a way to sell newspapers in this day and age?

Advertising also has a crucial role in enforcing gender stereotypes. DBS's 2022 regional ad campaign in Asia contains the slogan "More like mum's cooking, less like a bank"[23] – in this context, " mum" could easily have been replaced by "home". This is just one of the numerous ads which reinforce gender stereotypes across the world, including in the US, France and Australia[24].

If language bias is so endemic and a systemic part of our lives, thinking, and culture, how do we move forward and reduce bias in language?

Well, the good news is that language is never fixed. The English language has evolved continuously over 100s of years, borrowing and stealing words from other languages, and creating new ones, with words changing meaning as their usage in everyday life changes. It will continue to do

---

[22]Kipling, E. (January 17, 2023). "What Jeremy Clarkson said about Meghan Markle: 7 of the TV presenter's controversial comments". *Independent.* https://www.independent.co.uk/arts-entertainment/tv/news/what-did-jeremy-clarkson-say-about-meghan-b2263556.html (accessed February 10, 2023).

[23]Ragavan, S. (July 7, 2022). "Why DBS wants to be seen as a tech startup rather than a bank". *Campaign.* https://www.campaignasia.com/article/why-dbs-wants-to-be-seen-as-a-tech-startup-rather-than-a-bank/480167 (accessed February 10, 2023).

[24]Smoking Gun PR. (n.d.). "Gender divides: 8 incredibly sexist ads from this century". https://smokinggunpr.co.uk/gender-divides-8-incredibly-sexist-ads-from-this-century/ (accessed February 10, 2023).

so, and we can help expedite that change. We always have choices, especially with more than 170,000 words in the English language.

The bad news is some of this is so ingrained in our culture and so subtle we Don't always notice it, so it's probably not easy to change it quickly. But, there are some practical ways we can mind our language:

- Be mindful of the specific words and phrases we use daily. Do they contain bias – implicitly or explicitly? If yes, we should use them differently, switch them, or even make up a new word that doesn't have bias and encourage others to do the same.
- Use gender-neutral terms where possible. This won't completely eradicate society's gender bias, but it will help and at least encourage our young women to think about occupations without in-built assumptions of gender.
- Call out sexist or misogynistic comments when we hear them. Don't laugh along, Don't ignore them, and Don't let them slide. Explain why it's not appropriate. Was it necessary to use a gendered comment? Did the speaker even realise it was a gendered/biased comment? Change only happens when we're brave enough to challenge the status quo – although it might be that challenging is better-done one-to-one vs. in a large group to be most effective.
- Critique everything we read in the media, and be more mindful of the "click bait" we might encounter. Is that story "news", or just the media making money with a

ridiculous article designed to fill columns rather than fill your brain with anything useful? Is it fundamentally holding women to a different standard than men? Why? Can we call it out and stop it from being normalised?

- Think about how you interact with any children in your life. What do the words you use or that they're exposed to tell them about how they should act or behave and what they should value? Think about the messages you want them to hear and what you want them to place value on, and dial those up.

A heightened awareness of the biases language can contain is half the challenge. The higher your awareness, the more you will likely start to notice other examples you hadn't previously spotted – which is precisely what happened to me as I've been writing this chapter.

If we are all little more aware of what we say, what we read, and how we influence others with our language, and if we're just a little fussier about the words we use, if we pause to think a little before we speak to consider the meaning or subtext we might be conveying, then even if real change takes time, at least we're all heading in the right direction, to a more equitable future.

ABOUT THE AUTHOR

KAREN SCHOFIELD

Karen Schofield is a keynote speaker and trainer on happiness and resilience based in the UK. She is also on the Senior Leadership Team as Head of People at Blue Yonder Research, responsible for people culture and strategy, employee wellbeing, development, and rewards.

She has spent her more than 20 years career understanding the psychology of how we behave and how to influence it. For the last few years, she has specialised in happiness as an underlying driver of human motivation and its links to resilience. She has trained 100s of people in consumer psychology and resilience in SMEs, large Corporations and for industry bodies. She has lived in Europe and Asia, working across various sectors worldwide.

Karen combines professional knowledge with her own personal experiences of tragedy and resilience – and always with a touch of humour.

You can connect with Karen at:

Speaker profile on KeyNoteWomen.com:
https://keynotewomen.com/speaker/karen-schofield

: https://www.linkedin.com/in/karenschofield/

: http://www.karenschofield.co

STORY SIX

Thriving Amidst Chaos

The voice for those women that do not have a voice.

Let's journey through Afghanistan, a land of hope amidst chaos. The journey is full of lessons; lessons about strength, courage, perseverance, pushing boundaries and learning to restart over and over again. I have told this story many times, but this version is deeply personal. I have poured my heart into writing the following pages so that whoever reads it can live the journey.

The journey starts in Afghanistan's capital, Kabul, a name that brings fear in the hearts of many but brings a longing in mine – a longing to return. I was born in Kabul shortly before 9/11 in 2001. The 22 years I have lived thus far have always been associated with war.

Growing up, my mum told me many stories. Some stories were of the war and how it displaced her family. There were also stories about Afghanistan during the 1970s, when women studied at college freely and had the right, as citizens, to dress as they pleased, to lead their lives in the direction they desired, and had the opportunity to pursue careers that they found right. This Afghanistan is hard to imagine today when looking at the following pictures showcasing Afghanistan's drastic change.

Image: Afghanistan During 1970s (source: AFP)

Image: Afghanistan in 2022 (source: Reuters)

At 13, I was passionate about sports and music (and I still am). They allowed me to be expressive. My interests were also inspired by those around me who'd started breaking barriers. You see, for most of my lifetime, sports and music have been forbidden pursuits (especially for women) where I live.

My grandfather founded Afghanistan's first Symphony Orchestra before the first Taliban regime. His legacy is internationally acknowledged and respected. Under the first Taliban regime from 1996-2001, a dark era marked by extreme violations of fundamental human rights began. The regime banned music throughout the country and committed a historical and cultural genocide.

This lengthy period of conflict and extremist leadership transformed my homeland from a vibrant country populated with strong and independent women to a primitive society where women needed to fight for their rights continuously.

In 2001, the Taliban regime fell, but their five-year rule had already transformed many ideologies into extremism, making progress and development difficult. My mum was shocked by the changes – from college to lockdown, from miniskirts to burqa and mandatory headscarves, and from pursuing big dreams to pursuing nothing.

But I never knew any different. I was born and raised in a conservative society where women are not considered equals because they are a different sex. While external circumstances have transformed Afghanistan into a radical society over the past few decades, that radical society is not what defines Afghanistan. This land has nurtured intellectuality, poetry, science, history, and humanity.

Years after the Taliban regime fell, many Afghans, especially the younger generation, began pushing boundaries set during the dark eras of war. It was challenging, particularly for women. They had to fight against conservative and dark ideologies to return to politics, economics, journalism, music, sports, and more.

In 2009, my uncle, who received his PhD in Music from Monash University, returned to Afghanistan from exile in Australia. He started to make music accessible, not only because he was a musician and aimed to carry my grandfather's legacy, but also because music was a tool to help heal the nation after over two decades of trauma. His focus was mainly on the underprivileged class, but his bigger aim was to make music accessible to all students.

In 2010, he established the Afghanistan National Institute of Music (ANIM). Since music runs in my family, I joined the institute's Winter Academy programme in 2014. ANIM continuously thrived and nurtured young musicians, and by 2020, it had made Afghanistan the only place in the region with female orchestra conductors.

ANIM holds an annual concert at the end of the year. Some students also established rock bands outside of school which is how I was introduced to alternative rock and heavy metal. They played Metallica, Muse, Pink Floyd, and many more bands.

In 2014, some of these rock bands, White Page, District Unknown, Kabul Dreams, and a few more, held a concert in Afghanistan during the Sound Central Festival event, a regional alternative performing arts festival. This event was not solely for musicians but rather an opportunity for young people of different backgrounds to come together and share stories about how they are breaking cycles of conservatism and moving forward.

After the first band performed, everyone left the performance hall to network and grab a coffee. I was drawn to the various groups of dancers that were simultaneously performing at the back of the building.

There I noticed lots of bicycles propped against the wall. I had always loved cycling. As a child, my dad often took me bike riding and I would ride in front of our building. The sight reminded me of how I suddenly had to stop riding because I was a girl and I had become older and taller.

I excitedly approached the girls with the bicycles, and that was when I learnt about the Afghanistan Cycling Federation. To my great surprise, they had a women's team. I immediately asked how I could become a member, and with the coach's contact details in hand, I raced home to speak with my mum about joining the team. As much as she could see my excitement, she didn't agree for me to join.

My mum was involved in sports when she was my age, but considering the drastic changes in society, she was concerned. She didn't want to see me get hurt. After seeing me cry for two days, she caved in. We went and bought the appropriate attire, shoes, gloves, and helmet. My mum also spoke with the coach. That is where my fascinating cycling journey started. A couple of years later, I made it to the National Women's Team.

Image: Afghanistan's Women Cycling Team During Training (Source: Afghanistan Cycling Federation)

I met women from across the country as part of the cycling team. Some came from open-minded families that supported their sporting pursuits, while others were from conservative families who disapproved, so these women kept their sports lives hidden.

We usually trained together on weekends, travelling out of the city and into the countryside to avoid the nightmare of others watching and casting judgment. During the week, we couldn't train much, not only because of school and work responsibilities but also because not every member could afford a professional bike or cycling gear. I'm lucky, my mum bought a professional bicycle for me, and teammates from the men's team also supported me through training.

Every year, the federation held several competitions. The biggest event was in Nawruz, the New Year celebrated in

Afghanistan, Iran, Tajikistan, and other countries. Our Nawruz marks the beginning of spring, and the term translates into "New Day".

This competition was 580 kilometres, always starting in the capital Kabul and finishing in Mazar-e-Sharif, the regional hub of northern Afghanistan. This competition was incredible every year. Another major event we participated in was the annual competition in Bamyan, where provincial teams competed against each other in the beautiful Bamyan province with an altitude of nearly 3,000 metres, an ideal place for cycling championships.

Image: Annual Competition in Bamiyan

After several years, we realised the magnitude of our position in society; we were not only women in sports but activists as well, whether we liked it or not. We were pushing boundaries. Thus, we sought to strengthen our voices. We strived to be the voice of millions of other Afghan women. The beginning of our activism journey was the beginning of a whole new world of experiences for all of us.

In 2015, a horrific incident occurred in Kabul, which moved our team into action. A 27-year-old woman was stoned and beaten, and her body was set ablaze by angry men in front of a city centre mosque because she was falsely accused of burning the Quran. Her death sparked national and international outrage about women's rights in Afghanistan. To raise awareness, we organised a competition that started in the exact spot where she was killed, with her picture on our jerseys showing her bleeding, beaten face. All of us, as Afghan women, were heartbroken.

Image: Jaam-e-Farkhunda (Farkhunda Cup) Cycling Competition

Our sport and activism attracted various responses such as encouragement and words of motivation to horrible sentiments and even physical attacks. One of my teammates was riding at top speed downhill when two bodyguards unleashed their dog on her. She fell, was severely wounded, and now suffers a life-long spinal injury. Even after hearing her story, I never imagined anything could happen to me. I was very wrong.

During the month of Ramadan, our team typically trained at night (as it is difficult to train during the day when fasting). In 2016, after returning from the South Asian Cycling Championships in India, I went out to train with a teammate after breaking fast. We were riding along the airport road, and after we completed two circuits, a group of around ten men jumped in front of us. One of them pulled my bike and pushed me on the road with it. Thankfully, the cars on the main road stopped, and the situation didn't escalate. But the trauma and memory stayed with me for a long time. One moment my head was bleeding; the next, I woke up in the hospital. I was afraid to go cycling afterwards.

Surprisingly it was my mum who encouraged me to keep going. She emphasised it was up to me to choose whether to be a victim or a victor, and that I had the power to open the way for millions of other Afghan girls. That was precisely the motivation and encouragement I needed. As soon as I was well, I got back on my bike and continued training.

Shortly after, our team was nominated for the Nobel Peace Prize 2016 for our continuous efforts to empower women. It was a tremendous achievement, and we hoped this accomplishment would open more doors to Afghan girls and women.

Of course, our nomination sparked a lot of interest from the media. My coach usually sent me to do the interviews because I was the only one in the team who spoke English and German. In one of the interviews with the BBC, I stated that my biggest dream was to participate in the Tour de France, the world's most challenging cycling championship. I never imagined the interview would be watched by Mr and Mrs Giles, two cycling world champions who have won the Tour de France multiple times. Through the Secretary of the French Embassy in Afghanistan we were invited to participate in this prestigious cycling competition at L'Albigeoise in France. Mr and Mrs Gilles personally trained with us and provided us with new bikes and equipment. We placed second in the competition.

Image: Afghan Women Cycling Team on the Podium after L'Albigeoise

Our team continued to flourish. By the beginning of 2020, Afghanistan's Cycling Federation had 50 female members, making up over 50% of its members. Not only that, but the image of a woman on a bicycle was no longer nightmarish. A culture of cycling slowly emerged and it became common to see girls and women biking to school, work, and around the city. I am sure our team had a fundamental role in this development.

Image: Afghan girls and women on bikes (Source: Afghan Cycles)

Image: Afghan Girls and Women on Bikes in the City (Source: Afghan Cycles)

Despite all our hard work and accomplishments, our dreams were shattered in 2021 when the Taliban again took over Afghanistan. Immediately after their takeover, just like their first regime, they banned women from attending schools and universities and working. They have forbidden women from travelling without a male companion. Debates about music and sports are far from their agenda.

Given the Taliban's attitudes toward women and their cultural and historical genocides during the 1990s, many fled the country in horror. And today, once again, we are at a place where we can compare two pictures and interpret the damage that politics have caused. Yet again, in the 21st century, women are being erased from society and are at the frontlines of fighting for their fundamental human rights.

Image: Zawia Media Office in Kabul, February 2021

Image: Zawia Media Office in Kabul, August 2021

The pictures above are from Zawia Media, a media outlet I have been working for. Our CEO, Esmatullah Mohib established a digital media platform to portray Afghanistan from a distinct, fresh, unseen, and positive perspective. The platform shares efforts made by Afghans in building a better tomorrow and provides countless opportunities for Afghan women to contribute. When the Taliban entered Kabul in August 2021 they took over this company. Luckily, we could register it abroad, and the platform still functions.

Women continue to fight. Unlike under the Taliban's first regime, when women were locked inside their houses, this time, they are facing the Taliban, and they are striving not to let the world forget them.

Image: Women's Uprising Against the Taliban (Source: Los Angeles Times)

The above image shows women, some of whom are in their early twenties like me, and have similarly spent their lives pursuing their goals and dreams while facing the Taliban. This picture moves me because it shows how far the Afghan people have come despite the Taliban. These women are not afraid to fight for their fundamental human rights, like the right to study and work.

As I write this, over 500 days have passed since the Taliban banned women from attending all educational institutions. Today, more than ever, women need to be included because women are capable. Women have tremendous potential. We need to continue to be the voice for those women who do not have a voice. For our voices are the building blocks of equality and equity.

So together, let's speak up for a better and more inclusive tomorrow.

ABOUT THE AUTHOR

ZHALA SARMAST

Zhala Sarmast was born and raised in Kabul, Afghanistan. Her diverse interests range from

the sciences and philosophy to media, journalism, social activism, music, and sports.

Zhala is a member of Afghanistan's National Women's Cycling Team and has competed in national and international championships. Her cycling team has not only done well under the Afghanistan's National Olympic Committee, but the team has also been a symbol of courage and bravery. Zhala and her team were nominated for the Nobel Peace Prize in 2016. Zhala is also a member of the Afghanistan National Institute of Music's Guitar Ensemble.

Zhala holds a Bachelor of Science (with Honours) from Yale-NUS College, majoring in Chemistry, and she currently works for KeyNote Women Speakers and Zawia Media.

You can connect with Zhala at:

✉ : zhala.sarmast@u.yale-nus.edu.sg

in : https://www.linkedin.com/in/zhala-sarmast-4bab2917b/

STORY SEVEN

Embracing Equity Through Inner Work

Little changes in habits create big changes in lives.

"Who is this princess sitting in class," was all I could think of when I saw a girl, six years old, wearing a lavender tutu-style dress, satin ballerina-style pumps, and sparkling tiara in her hair.

It was 1988, during apartheid South Africa. Here I was, still within my first few weeks of starting pre-school, discovering someone different to me. Not just in her clothing, either. Her beautiful clear skin was dark in colour. Her lips were fuller, and her nose was flatter than mine. Her hair was very short but frizzy-curly. She was an African girl, the very first in my class. She stood out amongst the Indian children.

What I remember so vividly are her sparkly eyes. Even today, I still call her "Nandi with sparkling eyes".

It did not strike me at the time that she could be afraid, that this was a new and potentially scary environment for her, being the only African child in class. It also did not occur to me that she could still be lonely among us all. She was simply beautiful, and I admired her shyly from afar.

After about 30 minutes or so of shy surveillance and my thoughts flitting about her and fantasising about where she could be from, I noticed she was crying softly so that perhaps no one would notice. Until then, none of the children had gone up to her and spoken to her. It made me sad to see this little princess crying, so I stood up from my chair, walked over to her and said, "Hi! I'm Arthi. Please don't cry. You're so pretty".

Simple words that were straight from the heart. She looked

up at me with her tear-filled eyes and gave me a small smile. Again, I noticed something different about her, her dazzling white teeth. "Did I have teeth as white as hers?" I wondered. I made a mental note to check when it was bathroom break time. She thanked me and said she was wearing her birthday dress for school. It was not her birthday, but it was a special day and she dressed up.

She spoke eloquently, slightly lyrically, and our exchange went from expressing my desire to have a dress such as hers to "Could we sit together and do our activities?" to become firm friends. One by one, the rest of the class crowded around Nandi, questioning her about who she was, where she came from and why she was different from us.

This memory is vivid for me even today because of the many lessons and thoughts that have emerged over the years.

Some of my reflections on this include the following:

- The innocence of a child embracing novelty and differences with ease and happiness. I embraced Nandi for who she was, a child like me who looked different and spoke a different native language but whose second language, English, was British-English enunciation such that it, too, stood out.
- I didn't know about equality as a concept at that time. But I did know that Nandi was different to me. If anything, I didn't think she was less than me; I felt she was more than me, a princess. The freedom fight in South Africa centred around equality. And now, here was Nandi, a

testament to the move towards the fundamental right to education for all children, anywhere you choose, no longer predetermined or segregated because of your race or skin colour.

- Making the first move can be risky. But if your instinct points your compass in a particular way, trust yourself to follow it and see where it leads. My bravery in reaching out to Nandi allowed the other children to connect with her. Sometimes people hesitate, hoping to find someone or something to emulate, which offers them the courage to proceed.

It was historical and empowering watching my parents cast their vote for the first time in South Africa's first free and fair election in 1994. Through the courage and fight of brave men, women and children, the rest of the country took to the streets in numbers to make their voice for change heard by the simple act of voting in an election. Their collective courage was rewarded, as these elections brought a new guard, elevating the "rebel" African National Congress party into power with the late president Nelson Mandela at the helm.

The years that followed the euphoria of this crucial juncture in local and international history were tumultuous as we sobered into this reality of dismantling segregation and finding a way to heal. Equality, which had been a dream for so long, was achieved. But a newer insight was looming that equality was not enough; we needed equity as a nation to succeed.

In this light, the late Archbishop Emeritus Desmond Tutu convened the Truth and Reconciliation Commission in 1996 to help South Africans work through the deep-seated trauma, pain and suffering inflicted by actors of apartheid. The Archbishop knew this inner work was needed to embrace equity and unlock freedom and potential from the country's citizens.

These commission proceedings were televised, and I remember watching scenes of ordinary South Africans expressing with difficulty what had transpired to them and their families under the apartheid regime. I was filled with so many emotions, from anger to sadness to despair.

Watching these painful narratives unfold on television triggered another awakening, and I actively started studying my peers at school and in my community differently. The curtain had now been raised, the show was going on, and yet here I was backstage, witnessing and understanding the grittier side of people's lives in South Africa that I had not been exposed to before.

These social injustices I heard and saw left me with more questions than answers. I empathised with my African friends as we started to talk about their realities and hardships and our shared experiences as teenagers. What became stark was my privilege. I was privileged to have my family, with two parents in the household, an adult breadwinner, basic amenities within reach such as food, shelter, water, and the ability to have an education. Many of them could only count on having a couple of these.

As I journeyed toward embracing equity, my questions became sharp with my parents, teachers, and broader community members. Why were we perpetrating injustices that were meant to be dismantled? For example, I was uncomfortable with the language expressed towards different racial groups.

It was evident that racism resided within the community, honed by years of apartheid rhetoric aimed to mentally manipulate or brainwash an entire generation against specific race groups. Juxtapose this against the burden of upholding "Indian values" of how to behave and who to trust and not trust.

My burgeoning voice wanted to rage against the unfairness I heard and witnessed. Internally I did rant and shout. But externally, I remained neutral and did very little to "rock the boat". Like my friend Nandi, I was afraid to make the first move for fear of being ostracised by the community and ruining my family's reputation. Being that silent accomplice during that period has borne the effects of shame on me that my actions may have harmed others mentally and emotionally.

With this truth, I sought ways to work on my self-understanding. A large part of embracing equity is about embracing oneself. By chance, I took a psychology class at university which began my path to self-discovery.

When I entered the corporate world I was mentored by phenomenal businesspeople. They helped me test my boundaries and work through my fears and doubts. As a result, my career thrived and evolved. Another pivot point was undertaking a deliberate personal development module as part of my MBA programme that struck the core of me. At this point, I understood that deep inner work is crucial to unearth the ravages of what narratives like inequity do to us and shape our responses. Can you imagine the inner work needed to unravel the indelible scars on people based on the context of social and racial inequity? It is simply complex.

It still took years after my university, insights to acknowledge what embracing myself would be, look and feel like. It has been a rollercoaster of joys and trials. But the payoff of undertaking that difficult inner work still far exceeds those times of challenge and distress. Make no mistake, I am still on that roller coaster, enjoying the ride now because I am in tune with myself. This also permeates my work as a coach, as I assist others in finding their Prerna (inspiration), just as I have.

What, then, is Inner Work? Simply put, it is heightened self-awareness because of working through some difficulties and opportunities we have experienced. A seminal initiative is underway by the non-profit Inner Development Goals initiatives, where they "research, collect and communicate science-based skills and qualities that help us to live purposeful, sustainable, and productive lives" (www.innerdevelopmentgoals.org). While the intent behind the 23 qualities or capabilities that have been identified are aligned to achieving success in terms of the United Nations 2030 Sustainable Development Goals, these qualities also help us assess these capabilities for personal benefit.

Five key categories or pillars have been identified in terms of personal development. These include Being (relationship to self), Thinking (cognitive skills), Relating (caring for others and the world), Collaborating (social skills) and Acting (driving change). The Being and Thinking categories spoke to me directly.

I have been fascinated with how our brain is wired to function and what optimises its performance. The proven notion about our brain's plasticity means we have that direct means to enable change, incrementally or on a larger scale, based on our decisions. And our choices are primarily influenced by the mental models and narratives that have given us context since childhood until now.

We process all the information that comes our way, undertaking sense-making, critical analysis, and perspective unbundling, to name a few. Through these cognitive processes, we relinquish the priority our brain gives to unproductive or harmful routines and create or bring forward better ones.

Herein lies the link between inner development and the ability to embrace equity meaningfully. Only through knowledge and awareness of self can we begin to relate to others better through collaborative efforts that dismantle bias, spotlight blind spots to overcome them, and ultimately realise respect for the individual's uniqueness.

I've watched this play out and saw the benefits of this awareness for my personal journey. For example, in the 1990s, a number of tumultuous events rippled across the globe, such as the war in Iraq. The war created tensions amongst even my small community of Indian people. Suddenly distrust for those of the Muslim faith materialised, borne out of fear of terrorist and other violent attacks.

It became difficult for my Muslim friends, who were constantly pressured to defend their religion against this wave of mistrust. Attacks started to become personal, and being hormonal teenagers, situations became more charged than they should have.

Cliques started to form in school based on language and cultural differences. Tempers flared. My Muslim friends moved away from my group of friends, seeking a sense of belonging which they felt at that time that only their community could provide.

Belonging requires building psychological trust. A key takeaway for me at the time, and I still use this even more effectively today, is the inherent power of dialogue. Dialogue and genuine curiosity garner respect from those in the conversation. Respect leads to even more engagement and a sense of visibility. Both make people feel like they belong.

And in doing this process, one embraces the individual for who they really are. This leads to vital, possibly under-acknowledged benefits, which include:

1. **Intellectual capital** means those thoughts and ideas that could have the most significant impact can be shared. This cognitive diversity means unorthodox but feasible solutions could be implemented.

2. **Healthier discourse on crucial topics.** Active listening

allows one to elicit a profound understanding of another and respond with greater depth and perspective, thereby building trust.

3. **Equity improves transparency.** There are no hidden agendas, and a fuller picture allows robust decision-making and action.
4. **It builds agility** for yourself and those around you to thrive even in unpleasant circumstances.
5. **We become happier.** Humans are naturally social beings; the more we engage across a community, the more profound the impact created. Lasting impact is fulfilling and links to one's higher purpose potentially.

Here are some lessons I have learnt in embracing equity through inner work.

A. Foster the dialogue even if it may seem difficult.

This means communication needs to be a conversation, not a one-sided rant. It requires honesty, both in listening and talking. This is only possible if all parties in the process have undergone some inner work. In dealing with their truth, they can recognise, acknowledge, and applaud the truth of others.

B. Embrace the enemy of bias: feedback.

This does tie in with the dialogue mentioned previously. Biases occur due to the context of our upbringing and the social and cultural norms we are exposed to. These become the parameters and rules of engagement we work within to make sense of our world. But how often do we check these biases? How often do we audit whether our biases hinder or harm ourselves and others? One of the best ways to build up that check is through feedback from all types of people in our circles of influence and inference.

C. Upskill on how to use language effectively.

Words, actions, and silence enormously impact how we are perceived and how we hurt or enable others. The same words – said in different voices, tones, and pitch, with or without facial expression, little or many bodily gestures – can have profoundly different meanings to someone.

Our brain processes even the tiniest of cues and interprets them based on the manual we have stored in our memories. It finds patterns and associations and derives the "appropriate behaviour" for us based on that. However, this may not be best for us. Language triggers many emotions because of the meaning individuals attach to it, and it can be harmful in many ways if misused.

If we stall the natural urge to repeat patterns and instil a slightly more inquisitive nature or curiosity about the why and how to allow these patterns to be changed, it will help to overcome. This will lessen the negative impact on us and others too.

We can all play a part to shift the playing field to benefit us and those around us. Little changes in habits create big changes in lives.

**Names have been changed.*

ABOUT THE AUTHOR

ARTHI RABIKRISSON

Arthi Rabikrisson is a global award-winning ICF-certified leadership coach, featured and recognised across various global publications, including Finance Monthly, The NYC Journal and CIO Times.

She is the Founder and Managing Director of Prerna Advisory, a South African-based firm focusing on neuroscience-based coaching and assessment for individuals, teams and corporate organisations in South Africa and internationally. Arthi also consults on strategy for SMEs and is a capital introducer.

She is a key contributor and member of the Forbes Coaches Council and an opt-in member of the Advisory Council for the Harvard Business Review. Arthi's purpose is to inspire others to find their purpose towards impact.

Through mentoring, business coaching, keynote speaking, podcasts, training, and even as a board director, she strives to unlock a person's latent potential and harness it for personal and societal benefit.

You can connect with Arthi at:

Speaker profile on KeyNoteWomen.com:
https://keynotewomen.com/speaker/Arthi-Rabikrisson

: https://za.linkedin.com/in/arthi-s-rabikrisson-mba

: https://www.prernaadvisory.com

STORY EIGHT

Let's Talk About Sex, Baby!

Combat the awkwardness by starting the conversation early.

Sex has always been one of those topics that people cringe over or just want to ignore. As a teenager (largely thanks to perception), I saw the topic of sex as dirty, shameful and, to an extent, evil.

However, all that changed when I came across an article ten years ago where a study placed Sri Lankan teenagers ahead of the French when losing their virginity. The article stated that "while French teenagers would dabble in sex at the mean age of 17.5 (boy) and 17.2 (girl), Sri Lankan boys were already active at the age of 15.3 and girls at 14.4"[25].

Shocked/stunned/surprised, and whatever other words I could find in the thesaurus was my reaction.

Like most Asian countries, Sri Lanka boasts a conservative and sheltered culture regarding sociological issues like this. Naturally, the one question reverberating in my mind about the above-stated fact was, "Shouldn't it be the other way around?"

It all comes down to one word: CURIOSITY.

Lack of education, the unwillingness to speak about and normalise sex, and the stigma associated with breaking the cultural glass ceiling pushed these children into their voyage of discovery. This archaic way of thinking has many traditional countries convinced education will lead to activity. Well, guess what? They already are! And to top it off, there's very little to zero education.

---

[25]Patranobis, S. (April 1, 2009). "Lankan teens beat French in losing virginity". *Hindu Times.* https://www.hindustantimes.com/world/lankan-teens-beat-french-in-losing-virginity/story-ycvYNols8hZCkxKYLaWK8O.html (accessed August 9, 2013).

With my Sri Lankan heritage, I understood this as I was subject to the same culture of denial followed by the faraway voice echoing in my brain, " Don't do it!" What did I do as a kid growing up in Australia? I reached out to the only "experts" I could trust – my teenage friends. Girly giggles, introduction to sex slang and references to male genitalia as luncheon meat accompanied the information I got.

What was your first encounter with this taboo topic, my dear reader? A biology lesson? A naughty cinematic production? A raunchy song/dance/conversation? Or would you, too, rather not discuss it?

Most people still avert or have no idea how to start the conversation. Homes avoid it, schools ignore it, religion shames it, and the world has perverted it.

The reason why the modern youth are more curious about sexuality than any other preceding generation is that we live in a hyper-sexualised world. It is rare to see a movie devoid of some kind of nudity or sexual scene. Forget Hollywood. It's in the songs we listen to, the books we read and the advertisements we see.

Sex sells. Sex is everywhere, and we can't hide from it any longer.

There's a story about a ten year old girl who overheard some boys talking about oral sex on the school bus. She had never heard about it before, so when she got home, she immediately asked her parents, hoping to get some answers. Instead, her parents yelled at her and condemned her for asking such questions. So, she did what any young person today would do to find answers. She searched online and sadly was exposed to pornography for the first time. Imagine if only her parents had provided a safe space for their daughter to ask without fear and shame; how different would the outcome have been?

That story is about a girl in Australia. Yes. Forward, progressive, "western" Australia.

There is a school of thought that sex education programmes at the school level in the west are effectively comprehensive, primarily based on the fact that it's compulsory. In my view, that alone does not validate the competency of these programmes.

Belgium drew criticism for being extreme and not age appropriate by incorporating explicit sex positions in the syllabus for children as young as seven years old. The UK and New Zealand curriculums have been denounced as one-dimensional and limited with basic topics such as biology, dangers, and contraception.

The US-based programmes vary between schools and states with no formalised standard in keeping with emerging trends. Some states offer HIV awareness while other schools Don't teach birth control – neither of which captures the holistic nature of this vast topic.[26]

---

[26]Bilton, I. (November 9, 2017). "Sex education around the world: how were you taught?" *Study International.* https://www.studyinternational.com/news/sex-education/ (accessed February 1, 2023).

There is a global lack of equity in sex education between countries, so there is always room for improvement.

Curriculums need to evolve to include topics such as the power of sex, its consequences, peer pressures, the differences between males and females, relationships, pornography, consent and even the skills needed when facing major life decisions regarding your sexuality.

Sex has been watered down to the physical (sometimes animal-like or violent) act between people.

I respectfully disagree.

I believe sex is a beautiful thing. It can connect people in the most primal, intimate way.

Engaging all five senses, sex has the power to affect us on every level – physically, emotionally, biologically and even spiritually. If sex was just physical, why is heartache almost always associated with losing a sexual partner?

Why is it harder to break up when you've had a sexual relationship? Biochemically, a bond is created when two human beings engage in sexual activity. Literally, two are forged into one. A hormone called Oxytocin (OXY) is secreted in the brain.

OXY has been nicknamed the love or cuddle hormone. It is a chemical bonding agent in our bodies that creates pleasure, satisfaction and emotional closeness. A mother experiences it when she gives birth or nurtures a newborn, when an owner pets their dog and when people have sex. When there are high levels of OXY in either partner, they are predicated on overlooking points of contention. They can ignore the red flags, judgement gets clouded, and my dear reader, this is probably what birthed the phrase "love is blind"[27].

Just recently, a Sri Lankan university student slit his girlfriend's throat because he couldn't bear the thought of her being with somebody else after their breakup. He confirmed that she was his first sexual encounter, and he was hers.[28]

As painful as it is to hear stories like this worldwide, these are the stories that need to be shared – not for people to be fearful, but to show the emotional impact of sex.

The world is constantly changing, and if we Don't swim with the tide, we will end up drowning. That is precisely what has happened today. Parents, teachers and leaders have become overwhelmed.

It doesn't have to be scary.

We need to change the narrative, so this trend no longer continues. Fears, cultures and traditional beliefs have ensured a lack of sex education in schools. The focus is on

---

[27]Edwards, S. (2015) "Love and the Brain". *On the Brain*. Harvard Medical School, Publication Archives, Spring 2015. https://hms.harvard.edu/news-events/publications-archive/brain/love-brain (accessed January 28, 2023).

[28]Balasuriya, D.S. (January 18, 2023) "Girl murdered at Race Course Ground CCTV footage leads police to arrest suspect". *Daily Mirror*. https://www.dailymirror.lk/print/front_page/Girl-murdered-at-Race-Course-Ground-CCTV-footage-leads-police-to-arrest-suspect/238-252438 (accessed January 28, 2023).

how awkward it can be and not on how it can save lives.

I was recently finishing up a sex education workshop in Sri Lanka when one girl asked me a question. She wondered if abuse of any kind could affect other relationships that they might have. Of course, any sort of trauma and especially sexual abuse would affect future relationships. I realised with dread that the "someone" she mentioned was herself. With tears in her eyes, she shared how she had been sexually abused by her father when she was 11.

Eleven!

About 90% of perpetrators are known to the victim or family.[29]

Her own father. And it gets worse.

She continued to tell me that her father still lives in their home, and even though everyone knows about the abuse, everyone is in denial, and no one talks about it, especially her mother.

"I am so sorry," was all the comfort I could blabber, and her automatic response was, "It's ok".

I realised then and there that this was her coping mechanism. She had learnt to say this repeatedly because she had no one on her side, no one to believe in her or protect her, and she just had to be ok with it.

---

[29]Darkness to Light. (2017). *Child Sexual Abuse Statistics.* https://www.d2l.org/wp-content/uploads/2017/01/all_statistics_20150619.pdf (accessed January 27, 2023).

As much as I wanted to fix this, my hands were tied. Due to restrictions and lack of proof, all I could offer to support her was to connect her with a counsellor. With more awareness, we can shed light on this global issue. The point to take away from this is that this was possible because she attended a sex education class that didn't just teach her how to prevent it but gave her a safe space to share her story.

There has been much teaching on safe sex and the use of protection. With all the different types of contraception available, most have proven high rates of avoiding pregnancies, but with all these options, only one method boasts a 100% guarantee. You guessed it – no sex[30], which may not be popular or seem old-fashion, but youth need to be made aware of.

The salient question is; what are we protecting ourselves from? The standard and obvious answer is not getting pregnant, but it has to be more than that. No form of contraception is going to protect your heart and mind.

Mind you, just because you haven't gotten pregnant does not mean you're necessarily off the hook.

If you or your partner has been sexually active, there is a high probability of contracting a Sexually Transmitted Disease (STD). There are more than 20 STDs, and women are more at risk of getting an STD than men.[31]

---

[30]Planned Parenthood. (n.d.). *Birth Control.* https://www.plannedparenthood.org/learn/birth-control (accessed January 26, 2023).

[31]MedlinePlus. (2021). *Sexually Transmitted Diseases.* https://medlineplus.gov/sexuallytransmitteddiseases.html (accessed January 26, 2023).

Girls have been created with an open sexual system. Bluntly put, anything can penetrate the vagina. Boys are the dead opposite. Bluntly put, nothing can enter the penis.

Physiologically, this makes girls more prone to attracting an STD than males. Schools might teach about STDs but not explain how it affects a person – girls have more to lose. Some STDs Don't have symptoms in women, such as Chlamydia, so regular testing should be encouraged. If this bacterial infection is left untreated, it can lead to the possibility of being sterile. Viral STDs such as Genital Herpes is a lifelong ailment that never leaves. You won't die from it, but you must be careful as it can be transmitted to babies during a natural birth.

The most contagious STD, Human Papillomavirus (HPV), can lead to cancer. In the USA, there was a story of a 13-year-old girl who contracted HPV. By age 15, she had cervical cancer, and before her graduation, she had to get a hysterectomy. Imagine that outcome. All for want of some unguided, immature sexual freedom.

Testing and treatments for STDs Don't come cheap, which many teenagers Don't think about but should consider.

Unlike AIDS, which is transmitted by bodily fluid, blood and vaginal fluid, Herpes and HPV are transmitted through skin contact with genital areas.[32]

---

[32]Sharkey, S. (January 21, 2022). "Everything You Need to Know About Sexually Transmitted Diseases". *Healthline.* https://www.healthline.com/health/sexually-transmitted-diseases#causes (accessed January 26, 2023).

Did you know you can get many STDs without having intercourse? Again, it goes back to the fact that there is not enough focus on the consequences and how they can impact a young person's life – physically, emotionally and even financially.

Terrified? Forgive me, my intention is not to blacken your outlook on sex, but healthy fear is good. We fear fire, which is why we treat it respectfully; we enjoy its benefits. Sex is no different. There needs to be a balance between highlighting the positive side of sex and being brutally aware of the harmful and inconvenient side of sex.

Unfortunately, the lack of equity in sex education affects adults, especially parents, due to fear, ignorance or unawareness. As a mum myself I believe parents are the first educators in a child's life, and we need to be responsible for laying the foundation no matter the topic.

When a child hears something new for the first time, that becomes their foundation. Any information gathered after that will be compared to the original information received. This is why parents must fight to get to the front of the line, to be the first point of contact and provide all the information necessary for children to handle any situation that comes their way.

Combat the awkwardness by starting the conversation early. It's never too early to begin the birds and the bees talk. There is no exact age, but when they ask questions about their body or the things they observe, they are ready to start. Use the opportunities around you, such as the movies you watch or what they hear at school. Create a dialogue and ask them questions such as, "What do you think about the movie? How do you feel when you see a kissing scene? What does sex mean to you? Do you think other kids your age are watching pornography? Is it ok to share intimate photographs with another person?" Remember talking about sex isn't a one-time chat but many conversations you'll have with them as they grow up.

Inadequacy might play a big role in warding you off-topic as this world is constantly changing but stay the course. The only way to be ahead of the curve is to resource yourself, and if there is something you Don't know too much about, be honest with your kids. It's ok not to know and to be open with them. When you need time, take the time to research and make sure you come back to them to continue the conversation.

Reassure them to direct any questions to you as their parents rather than asking Uncle Google or Aunty TikTok.

Affirmation is a big key to having great conversations. When we encourage them by saying, "I'm so glad you asked me that", it will make your children come back to you with more questions. As parents, it's not just about answering their questions but equipping them with the tools to place boundaries for their protection and discussing the negative impacts of this topic instead of just sweeping it under the carpet.

Regardless of your faith or race, everyone deserves and has the right to sex education so they can be empowered:

- To have a voice of their own instead of others speaking on their behalf.
- To have all the necessary information in their hand so that they can make healthy decisions regarding their sexuality and relationships.
- To have confidence in themselves to stand for what is right and believe they can positively influence this world.

Let's change how we think about sex, stop focusing on the awkwardness of the topic and see it as lifesaving. Remember, knowledge is power. Instead, let's not only imagine but start bringing change so that there is equity in sex education, whether at home, in schools or in our governments, where our children are more aware, wiser, assertive and fully equipped to succeed in this life with no regrets especially when it comes to their sexuality.

***"Do not accept that which you can't change.
Change what you cannot accept".***

– Angela Davis

ABOUT THE AUTHOR

MANEESHA BENEDICT

*Maneesha Benedic*t is a speaker, advocate, educator and leader. As a wife and mother, she is passionate about women's and youth empowerment and inspires them to fulfil their purpose. She grew up in Sydney, Australia, where she completed a Bachelor's degree in Applied Science and a Master's in Arts.

Now residing in Sri Lanka, Maneesha is the Managing Director of KeyNote Women Speakers, which promotes and supports women speakers globally. She also founded Gen.u.in, a platform dedicated to removing the stigma surrounding the topic of sex. Its mission is to empower young people to make healthy decisions regarding relationships, sexuality and life.

Maneesha also has a children's book coming out soon to help parents start the conversation about sex. She believes parents are the first educators of a child's life and aspires to equip them to be able to guide their children in this hyper-sexualised world.

You can connect with Maneesha at:

✉ : maneesha.benedict@gmail.com

in : https://www.linkedin.com/in/maneesha-benedict-8a11bb218/

◎ : https://www.instagram.com/gen.u.in/

STORY NINE

Why Science Needs the Female Angle

Believe in yourself and get out of your comfort zone.

I'm a scientist by training as well as a scientist at heart. I believe in using technology to overcome pressing global challenges and positively shape the future of our planet.

I grew up in Germany and fell in love with the sciences. At university, I studied biology and chemistry. I stuck to science and research for my PhD, postdoctoral years, and my first 10 years in the industry.

I realised that not everyone shares my passion for biotech. I´ve encountered environmental groups that brand biotech as non-natural and dangerous throughout my career. They raise fears amongst the general public and pressure governments to increase regulatory requirements that slow down or even prevent critical solutions to global agricultural and food challenges. Why?

Rejecting technology is tragic. Biotech is part of the solution.

As a chemistry student at Stanford in the early 1990s, I used to bike across the beautiful Stanford court, which featured a wonderful view of the foothills. Stanford's town hall meetings on gene technology were emotional discussions on the pros and cons, an environment that taught me to stand up for my beliefs and to dedicate my life to something that matters.

Since my summer student internship at the Department of Genetics in Cambridge, UK, this "what matters" was biotechnology. What else? Being a vegetarian since I was nine years old, I did not see myself killing lab animals to do cancer or vaccine research, and therefore, I chose plants as my lab rat and PhD topic.

In the late 1990s, I was working on my thesis in Berlin. I used biotechnology to produce potatoes with beneficial traits that conventional methods could not achieve. However, our first field trials with these genetically optimised potato plants became a controversial public issue.

I'll never forget helping with planting tubers on the vast plains of Brandenburg, which has sandy soil perfect for potatoes as demonstrators desperately interfered. They didn't understand breeding or genetics. They didn't consider the benefits of improving potato breeding. They were convinced we were doing the wrong thing without even having a dialogue with us. They were loud, outraged and emotional.

Emotions sell. The public bought into the emotions of the protestors and grew concerned over the trials.

We harvested the tubers later that year, but the public outrage affected me deeply. The protests convinced me to stay the course because I truly believed in the benefits of biotechnology; I knew these plants and the technology were safe. This event helped me to become a tenacious, vocal proponent of biotechnology.

In a recent podcast, I was asked about being female. I thought, "Well, yes, I am a woman. So what?" Shortly after, I was chatting with my friend, a psychiatric medical doctor, about writing this personal story on gender equity for International Women's Day. She replied, "That's exactly it!"

"What is?" I asked, not getting her point.

"You have no idea what is special about being a woman in

your field". She explained that most women experience some kind of reservation or self-discrimination that can hold them back.

"You Don't . You never did", she confirmed.

I feel lucky to have inherited this trait from my mum, a traditional housewife with four kids (me being number 3) - confident, fearless and free-spirited. My part in it was taking this spirit to the world.

From my inner experience, there might be little difference between genders in biotech. From my outer experience, I see some good and bad differences.

On the one hand, being female brought me success in leadership, networking, advocacy and visibility. When I was Head of Research and later Head of Government Relations in a big corporation, my groups consistently outperformed other groups and achieved extraordinary results.

I selected and pushed strong, independent-thinking people; freeing up their time to research, advocate, and support them to get their jobs done. The idea that high performance, success and maintaining a warm, friendly atmosphere are not contradictions, but the true essence of leadership may be easier to embrace for women. My "soft" social skills, typically seen as female traits, have also allowed me to negotiate in environments where my male colleagues had been unable to move projects forward, such as opening up markets for specialty food ingredients in China.

Other positive reactions included being declared a "Female

Food Hero" by CropLife International for my long-standing engagement and impact on food and agriculture innovations or being invited as a keynote speaker or key panellist at international biotech or nutrition conferences.

On the other hand, the 24 years of outstanding work achievements, immense visibility throughout the company up to the Board level and constant positive evaluations never translated into the promotions that my much-less-successful male colleagues enjoyed. Here, the same qualities that made me shine on the international stage – being unafraid to speak out, to name problems, and to push for solutions – became roadblocks on my career path. I was seen as too energetic, too strong, and too successful in the outer world – in other words: too unfeminine.

I am not only a scientist. I´m also a woman and mother. Some parts of society think this gives me a natural right to talk about what's good for mother nature and future generations. By my appearance alone, NGO members demonstrating against plant biotechnology were convinced I was one of them. One of them? One of those concerned about biotechnology and have reservations against progress without good reasons?

At first, when this started happening, I was astonished. How funny they see me as an anti-technology warrior. But then I accepted it and became active in speaking for biotechnology, both in public and policy. It's a matter of imagination and storytelling. And about authenticity.

The Founder and Chair of KeyNote Women and my former colleague told me in one of her master classes on speaking in the virtual world that she is frequently using me as an example of the power of imagination. I was surprised. But then she reminded me of when she watched me run a highly controversial podium event on plant biotechnology with an organic farmer, a representative from an NGO, and a Green party representative.

That day, I was set up to be "the bad guy". I was the sole industry representative. Somehow, I won the hearts and minds of the crowd. Even the podium members nearly forgot they did not favour plant biotechnology. What had happened? I arrived at the auditorium on a yellow bike, pregnant, wearing colourful clothing, and feeling happy. On stage, I smiled, was friendly, authentic, supportive, highly competent, and not at all what the audience or panellists had expected.

This shows the power and importance of having women in biotech. I am not big on chemistry, but I represent the female scientist who believes in a wonderful future. Unfortunately, there aren't enough of us. I´ve spoken at dozens of town halls, conferences and various events, convincing thousands of people, including NGO representatives and organic farmers, about the bright future I see for biotech. My mission is not over. I have more to do. And getting more female ambassadors on board is crucial.

Staying on Course and Broadening your Opportunities

I studied biology at a time when nobody had an idea what to do with it except be a nature guide. Or becoming a taxi driver. With undertones of criticism and astonishment, I was constantly asked, "What do you want to do with it?" I replied:

"I Don't know yet, but I enjoy it". Fellow students dropped out left and right, switching to medicine or passing their teaching exams to work towards a secure, well-defined job. I never worried about earning a living. I pursued a topic I loved.

When I started as a KeyNote Speaker, I planned to talk solely about biotechnology and how it could advance the public good. I wanted to share how biotech helped develop plants with a higher yield, pathogen resistance, and tolerance of abiotic stressors or how precision fermentation produces vitamins, enzymes, oligosaccharides and aroma for sufficient, healthy nutrition and well-being.

However, the KeyNote Women community and its masterclasses taught me that speaking for biotech is not only about fighting regulatory constraints and opening markets. I could also share my views on technology friendliness, sustainability concepts, growth mindsets, and X-shaped changes for disruptive product innovations.

Suddenly I had a bigger audience I could inspire, inspiring me in return. What is most wonderful, if you put yourself out there and are on the move, more doors open, and more opportunities present themselves. Over the past several years, saying "yes" to requests for which I did not know where they might lead allowed me to give serendipity a chance. As a result, I met wonderful people, expanded my networks, got new ideas, gained personal strength, and increased my professional impact.

Pouring your energy and excitement about a topic into corporate innovations for over 24 years runs the risk of depleting your energy. When I looked around for sources of inspiration for myself as a person, I met a future coach who offered an extensive programme in dealing with the future using trend reports of sectors like energy, health, mobility, nutrition and housing, as well as topics like virtual reality and blockchain, plus methods to picture yourself in this future and a community of future-loving people for support.

I deeply reflected on myself, my interests, and my behaviour patterns and kept thinking for several months. This allowed me to confirm my future in biotech, innovation and sustainability but changed my focus away from working within one big corporation to helping many companies reach their product goals.

This decision has been incredibly refreshing and encouraging. In addition, I decided to create financial security for this new path by working with a money management coach and doing an investment education programme. My goal is to develop investment and stock management skills that will ensure my long-term financial security and independence so that I can choose work that energises me and that will contribute the most to solving global problems for a sustainable future.

Think about your future. Do a thorough analysis of your potential "future me". Create several options. Decide against individual options one by one until you have filtered them down to a few. Let the concepts sink in. Feel where your heart goes.

Select one “future me”. This is the target you want to reach in the next three to five years. Find a community that critically reflects on you and positively encourages you. Make a plan in your calendar to stick to the plan. Implement your plan and revisit it. This cycle should be repeated every five years. New beginnings are magical. You always start on a higher level than last time.

Learn healthy selfishness. Don’t be afraid to rock the boat, even when you are the only one. Don’t run around pleasing everyone. Don’t take everything personally. Do what is right for you. Don’t compare yourself with others, but with your past self and the self, you envision in your future.

My friend, a Professor in Biology and an Author cited me from when I was attacked and severely criticised for following my mind during our time together as postdoctoral students: “This accusation is so absurd, I can’t possibly worry about it”. When I asked her now to challenge me on my purported future me, she was relaxed and said: “Elke, wherever you are is a supernova”. Know yourself. Trust yourself. Enjoy yourself.

Think bigger. Then you will reach bigger targets. Can I, a biologist, apply for a Chemistry Scholarship at Stanford? I tried it – and won. Can I, a biotech expert from Germany, really convince the authorities around the globe to open the markets for biotech products? I tried it – and won often. Find an angle, find a hook. Just do it. You will win; even if you Don’t , the process is a valuable experience.

Strive for financial independence. I only recently learnt how essential it is to change my attitude towards money, and to love money, not for taking a Dagobert Duck-style money bath, but for the good I can do with it and whom I can support. You need money to be free and secure, to keep yourself and your family. This security makes a big difference. I am not there yet, but I have started to educate myself, enter an investor community, take ownership, and make decisions for my money management. Do not let a bank accountant or your partner do this for you. Do it yourself. Take ownership of your financial accounts – it is possible to do this positively.

Environment matters. Fulfilment at work and financial independence are core to a happy life. Don't wait for others to make you happy, but choose the right environment, especially in times of inner and outer growth. Look for a community to influence your mindset and broaden your horizon.

Once you have created the space where you can grow, you will feel comfortable as you speak on big stages, love the future, or talk about money and investments. You will feel at home. This sense of belonging is an incredible motivation and will give you strength and authenticity, whatever is out there.

Look for role models. I do not have a particular role model myself, but I always had great individuals, often females, around me that encouraged and supported me. And I always had great individuals, usually females, around me that I encouraged and supported, both in my professional and private lives. I actively lecture in schools and universities for a career in STEM.

Check out. I entered the corporate world to work on biotechnology, develop new products, and bring them to the market. I have been with a big corporation for 24 years. As an independent advisor, I can fulfil my vision of supporting biotech products in the market. If your career leaves you unhappy, check out of that path and look for something else. Put your eggs into another basket for mental and physical health and for being the productive and happy person you deserve to be.

Just do it! When offered the opportunity to write this article, I felt uncomfortable as the topic and format were new. Then I remembered what I said to other people: "Just do it. Believe in yourself and get out of your comfort zone. Now!"

What's my learning? Walk the talk. Look for opportunities to grow. Say "yes" before you know how to do it. It will work. You will make it work.

ABOUT THE AUTHOR

DR ELKE DUWENIG

Dr Elke Duwenig is a biotechnology expert, scientist, keynote speaker, and consultant in strategy and policy work.

Elke is passionate about innovation and sustainability. She is safeguarding biotech products, opening markets and shaping legislative and regulatory frameworks globally, both for plant and microbial biotechnology and precision fermentation. She supports biotech products from the first idea through R&D to successfully bring them to the market, and is committed to embracing technology for a great future.

Elke is a senior Regulatory & Government Affairs expert at Nutrition & Health, BASF.

She studied biology and chemistry at the University of Münster, Germany and Stanford University, USA. Elke graduated in molecular plant physiology at IGF (Institut für Genbiologische Forschung) in Berlin. Before joining the industry as Head of Research and later Head of Government Relations for plant biotechnology at BASF Plant Science, she completed two postdocs at MPI (Max-Planck-Institute) in Golm and Freiburg University, Germany.

You can connect with Elke at:

Speaker profile on KeyNoteWomen.com:
https://keynotewomen.com/speaker/elke-duwenig

: https://www.linkedin.com/in/elke-duwenig-0984917

: https://www.drelkeduwenig.com

STORY TEN

Money is Not a Dirty Word

Only you can take charge of your finances.

I met Maria* at a job interview in Mayfair, London's most affluent neighbourhood. She wore a purple dress and sat back relaxed, stockinged legs crossed. I perched uncomfortably on the edge of my seat in an ill-fitting blouse and a new Marks & Spencer navy suit.

Gripping her printed CV, I asked, "Can you share an example of a complicated travel itinerary you planned?" and nervously glanced at my boss for reassurance. I was in the early years of my career, working as an HR assistant at an investment firm, and this was my first time interviewing – under the severe supervision of my superior. We were hiring a senior executive assistant for the business development team.

Maria snickered. Her tight curls, thickly gelled, bounced in unison. Smoothing the woollen skirt of her dress with a well-manicured hand, she coolly listed her extensive experience organising international roadshows for several global asset managers. I frantically scribbled notes to avoid eye contact. What a fraud I felt! Here I was rattling off scripted questions to a woman more experienced and well-put-together. Even my boss, who rarely gave compliments, applauded Maria's impressive track record. We offered her the job that same day.

She was a brilliant assistant. With no training and little ado, Maria took charge of schedules and brought order to chaos. She navigated international time zones like a fluent second language. And when she planned an event – an investor lunch or casual office party, she'd scrutinise every detail right down to the wine list.

We operated in a fast-paced environment. Tempers flared, and last-minute crises arose all the time. I often found myself cowering behind the safety of the computer screen. Maria didn't hide. She raised her voice and maintained composure and professionalism at all times.

As it happened, Maria, the new employee, took me, the so-called HR professional, under her wing with a crash course on working for the buy side. She briefed me on the management structure of our competitors, explained what different departments actually did, and, most importantly, gave lessons on how to motivate and influence others (otherwise known as getting shit done when senior people ignore your emails). We became close friends.

Maria was equally brilliant outside of office hours. She lived in a fabulous Soho apartment with bohemian rugs and Moroccan lamps, drank Vesper Martinis, had a personal salsa instructor, and flaunted an incredible array of crazy hats. All while being employed on a temporary contract.

"Why Don't you insist on becoming permanent?" I'd nag. And I quizzed her about progressing beyond administrative work. She had the savvy to climb the corporate ladder. Maria always dismissed me with a wink, as though I were a silly child, explaining contract secretarial work was so much more lucrative. I could hardly argue; her salary was nearly double mine.

Time passed. Maria moved on. I continued building an HR career, and we caught up less and less. In 2017, I got a big job promotion and relocated to Singapore. We completely lost touch. I didn't hear from her again until 2021.

"I'm desperate," her voice cracked over the phone. She didn't sound like the composed Maria I knew.

The Pandemic was raging, and Maria was unemployed. She couldn't afford to pay rent. She still lived in the same eclectically furnished Soho apartment which, she cried, she couldn't "bear losing" while everything else fell apart.

At first, I felt pity. I felt disgusted. And I felt angry that she would dare ask me for money, so I hung up the phone. But then I thought some more about it. How did a capable woman, who'd spent over a decade working in financial services, end up in such a terrible position? Maria had earned a comfortable wage. She'd worked closely with some of the most successful investment professionals in the industry. She was intelligent. But she didn't know anything about saving or investing. She lacked the right skills and values to manage her finances.

Women are Poorer than Men

Women have made significant progress in areas such as work, education, and politics over the past 50 years. But we are still poorer than men. Why?

On average and across the globe, women earn less money, hold fewer high-paying positions, and experience more career interruptions compared to men[33]. These factors, which

[33] Willis Towers Watson. (2022). 2022 Global Gender Wealth Equity Report: The role of gender in wealth equity. *WTW*. https://www.wtwco.com/en-US/insights/2022/11/2022-global-gender-wealth-equity-report (accessed January 26, 2023).

equate to lower lifetime earnings, are further compounded by lower financial literacy rates in both advanced and emerging economies[34]. This means women are less likely to save money, invest in the stock market, diversify risk, successfully manage unexpected financial hardship, and accumulate wealth than men. According to the current global Wealth Equity Index, women are only expected to accumulate 74% of the wealth that men have in their lifetime[35].

These numbers Don't even reveal the whole story. Many women remain financially dependent on men, even in the developed world, but are captured as better-off on paper when living in households with their male partners or family members[36]. And just as many women look to men for guidance or management of their finances. I'm part of several women's Facebook groups, and every month a new post appears that goes along the lines of:

Anon.

Hi ladies. Divorce lawyer with strong financial knowledge needed. My husband has always managed our finances. I haven't seen a bank statement in years and have no idea what we own in stocks or how to access any of this. Need help to find out my exact situation and rights.

---

[34]Hasler, A. and Lusardi, A. (2017). The Gender Gap in Financial Literacy: A Global Perspective. *Global Financial Literacy Excellence Center.* https://gflec.org/wp-content/uploads/2017/07/The-Gender-Gap-in-Financial-Literacy-A-Global-Perspective-Report.pdf (accessed January 30, 2023).

[35]Willis Towers Watson. *ibid.* 5.

[36]Williams, A. (2021). *Why Women Are Poorer Than Men and What We Can Do About It.* Penguin Random House, Ebook Library, 11.

Consider yourself. Are you financially savvy? How would you rate your financial well-being today? Perhaps you are on top of these matters. What about your female friends and colleagues? How do they fare?

I'm like Maria

I was quick to judge Maria when she asked me for a loan. The truth is, I'm no better. Just luckier.

I moved to the UK in my twenties with nothing more than a suitcase, a loud Aussie accent, and a few thousand dollars in the bank. Eight years later, I left with two suitcases, a strange East End-inspired twang, and barely much more in savings. I had established a career, and my salary was higher than I ever dreamt it could be. But I also had a severe case of the travel bug. You can't blame me; Australia really is the end of the Earth. Hiking across Turkey, a snowy Christmas in Iceland, and island hopping in Greece were some of my marvellous adventures.

My first marriage was also an expensive affair.

Three weeks after moving to London, I fell for the smartest man on the planet. Maksim, a rugged Russian, was well-versed in European history. He loved a few beers and vodka even more.

We discussed classic literature for hours on end. He showed me Dickens' London and introduced me to off-licences and Lambrini (Don't ask).

Within a year, we wed. Maksim didn't work. I supported us

financially – the rent, the bills, the holidays, and the drinking. But we were happy. It was London. Everything seemed possible. Who cared about money?

Well, I eventually ended up in Singapore, and suddenly nothing seemed possible. As a foreigner, I constantly worried about job security, rising rents, and if my work pass would be renewed. The marriage didn't work out.

One day, I met a friend for a coffee which changed my life.

Sharon, a senior executive and fellow Singapore expat, didn't know what to do with her savings. Between slurps of frothy latte, she moaned to me about her useless financial advisor and asked, “Where are your investments?”

“Uh, what investments? I'm not an investor”.

Her jaw dropped. “But what if you're in an accident and have to retire early? How will you look after yourself?”

At 35, this was my first real conversation about personal finance.

Fed up with wily advisors, Sharon embarked on a financial literacy journey to take matters into her own hands. She studied various financial instruments, researched product offerings (and the associated fees) offered by all the major banks, and evaluated digital advisors and other online investment apps. She also shared her learnings with me. Listening to Sharon was the inspiration I needed to take control of my situation.

Money is not a Dirty Word

Finance is not a realm reserved for business leaders, investment professionals, or bankers. Financial literacy is an essential life skill. More women can learn how to protect and grow their wealth.

Financial concepts are complicated; it's as if the system is difficult by design to limit popular participation. What's more, financial literacy is more than just numbers and terms. It also relates to behaviours and attitudes towards money, often ingrained from childhood. So what can we do to improve the status quo for ourselves and others?

The first and easiest step is to realise money is not a dirty word. We can and must discuss financial topics openly with our partners, family, friends, and children. Be like Sharon. Interrogate the females in your life about their financial well-being. Conversation leads to normalisation and increased awareness which in turn drives better financial literacy.

Only you can take charge of your finances. There are resources available if you Don't know where to start. In her book, Williams sets out a foundational guide[37] for achieving financial resilience. There is also the Asia-based platform, Sophia[38] which provides female-focused financial education for women wanting to future-proof their lives.

---

[37]Williams, A. *ibid.* 183-189.

[38]Sophia. (2003). https://www.sophiawomen.com/ (accessed February 1, 2023).

Finally, teach these crucial life skills to younger generations. If you have children, or nieces and nephews, demonstrate how to budget, save, and spend responsibly. Help them to invest and track investment performance together. It's a great bonding activity.

Williams said it best, "Putting money aside today shows that you care about your future self as much as you do about your current self... One day, your 75 year old self will be grateful you were thinking of them today ".[39]

I'll take that one step further and add we're in it together. Let's show we care not only about our future selves but also the prospects of other women and those we care about. Let's talk about money.

My Wish List

When I was eight, my parents opened a savings account for me with St George Bank. The clerk gave me a golden dragon-shaped money box, which I cheerfully filled with one and two-dollar coins. It took about six months to fill my dragon to the brim, after which I'd proudly march to the local branch with mum and dad to deposit my treasure trove.

At 14, my father gave me a choice. On weekends, we could go out and do fun stuff together, and he would pay for any food or costs incurred. Or, I could receive five dollars a week in pocket money, and I'd be responsible for funding my weekend treats.

---

[39]Williams, A. *ibid.* 183.

This was the extent of my financial education. We didn't discuss money at the dinner table. I didn't learn much about financial concepts at school; interest and compound interests were simply formulas we memorised for maths.

I feel foolish for not taking better financial care of myself earlier in life. For my children's sake, I hope finance will be part of formal school curriculums one day. Some schools in the US and other developed countries are already doing this. We need governments to drive such a strategy forward and provide leadership, incentive, and coordination across educational institutions. Children have a right to grow up with the ability to make sound financial decisions.

As an HR practitioner, of course, I have a wish list for corporates as well.

We all work to earn a living and provide for our families. We deserve the ability to use our income to realise financial freedom later in life. This notion should be driving corporate benefits strategy, and I'd like to see multinational corporations step up and set the gold standard.

Benefits packages must deliver real value. Provide opportunities for employees to improve their financial literacy and confidence. Give employees access to investment advice. Teach them how to plan for financial security. Empower your people to grow their earnings so they can fund what matters most at whatever stage of life they are at.

Finally – and this is the big one – I wish all large corporations contributed to employee pension plans. Today, this only happens in some economies. Employer contributions are not a statutory requirement for all employees in all countries and usually, it is the part-time, low-income, and foreign workers who miss out.

Every country in the world has a gender pension gap in favour of men[40]. Women's pensions are lower due to career breaks and lower salaries. Women are also more likely to perform part-time work (either due to personal choice or to accommodate caregiving responsibilities); temporary or contract workers are not eligible for many corporate pension schemes.

Obviously, multinational corporations cannot own global pension reform. But they can significantly reduce the gap by contributing to all employee retirement schemes, including for part-time workers and workers on maternity or parental leave.

In short, well-paid and happy employees translate to better productivity for corporations. Multinational corporations have the budget to take the lead on evolving benefit strategies. If they do, I'm certain they'll see a fair return on their investment.

I Don't know what happened to Maria. The phone number was disconnected when I tried calling her back, and she'd vanished from social media. I wish I'd been more empathetic.

---

[40]Mercer. (2022). *Mercer CFA Institute Global Pension Index 2022.* https://www.mercer.com/our-thinking/global-pension-index.html (accessed February 4, 2023).

There is a lot we can all do and wish for. Most of all, I hope my stories have motivated you to take control of your finances today.

**Names have been changed.*

ABOUT THE AUTHOR

SARA KELLY

Sara Kelly is a Human Resources specialist and creative writer. Based in Singapore, her diverse background includes over ten years in various HR positions covering European and Asia Pacific regions and leading global projects. A master of observation – she writes non-fiction articles about her working experiences, expat life and parenthood, authors a children's poetry site, and regularly performs at spoken word events.

Sara's professional and creative work is driven by her desire to challenge perceptions and turn the status quo upside down. Financial equity is one issue she has cared deeply about since becoming a volunteer with Aidha – a charity empowering and providing opportunities for low-income women to transform their lives through sustainable wealth creation.

Sara holds a BA in Media & Communications from the University of NSW, Australia and an MA in Creative Writing from LASALLE College of the Arts, Singapore.

You can connect with Sara at:

✉ : sarapatriciakelly@gmail.com

in : https://www.linkedin.com/in/kellysara/

STORY ELEVEN

Decoding Discomfort to Recondition Oneself

Looking inward to move forward.

While many Indians (62%) say that men and women should play an equal role in childcare, roughly 34% feel childcare should be handled primarily by women[41]. Since the Pandemic, an increasing number of female employees in India have quit their jobs to cope with family responsibilities.[42]

If you had told me 20 years ago that I would quit a successful career as a senior technology consultant to raise a family and support my spouse, I would have pounced on you. But that's what happened. In 2013, I resigned. I wasn't asked to quit by my family. The decision was mine.

And, if I hadn't left back then, I would have surely done it in 2020 during the Pandemic.

Quit because the Pandemic challenged women to stay employed and productive at work while managing their homes. Especially women like me, the ambitious and balanced females of the 21st century. Balance for me is the ability to excel in two of my roles, one being the COO (Chief Operating Officer) of my household and two being the primary carer for my child. A shinier phrase for the above two roles is a loving mother and an excellent homemaker.

---

[41]Pew Research Centre. (2022). *How Indians View Gender Roles in Families and Society. Pew Research Center.* https://www.pewresearch.org/religion/2022/03/02/how-indians-view-gender-roles-in-families-and-society/ (accessed January 10, 2023).

[42]Majority of women say family responsibilities prompted them to quit their job. (2022). *The Economic Times HRWorld.* https://hr.economictimes.indiatimes.com/news/workplace-4-0/diversity-and-inclusion/majority-of-women-say-family-responsibilities-prompted-them-to-quit-their-job/90157699 (accessed January 10, 2023).

If I was also working full-time during the Pandemic, I would have become drained. I adore being a homemaker and a mum, but I also abhor being burdened by it. The Pandemic caused me to reflect on my earlier decision to prioritise family responsibilities over career.

Deep-seated beliefs I had about domestic responsibilities are at the core of such reflection. For many years I thought women should be responsible for the home. Have you been in a position where your domestic expectations weighed you down?

Phew! I am not alone. In some ways, it is a relief to realise the burden is self-imposed. Alas! How long it took me to realise this simple fact. What is not so simple, however, is what made me stick to my core belief that women had to be in the frontline at home for many years. I still cannot believe that I had belief perseverance, a tendency to cling to one's initial belief even after receiving new information that contradicts or disconfirms the basis of that belief.

What You Resist Persists

My beliefs were intrinsically linked to my cultural upbringing. I grew up in Chennai, Southern India, surrounded by women who were exceptional homemakers. I observed the women tending to all the home needs, cooking the food, caring for children, and hosting guests.

Southern Indian women are more highly educated than their counterparts in India's Hindi Belt. But Southern adults are more likely to believe that women should be primarily responsible for taking care of children (44% vs 30%). Also, Indian women are only slightly less likely than Indian men to say they completely agree that wives should always obey their husbands (61% vs. 67%)[43].

My mother is a multi-faceted lady. She was a banker, dressmaker, beautician, singer, and a fantastic cook all at the same time. She had an astonishing ability to skilfully manage work and home and make time for her passions. I remember her going from a plain-looking hardworking mother in the day to a shiny attractive singer in the evening. She rose early, fixed our breakfast and lunch before she left for work, carried heavy bags of kitchen supplies on her way back home, fixed meals, performed at events as a singer, and tended to my dad's health needs. She has always been independent and fearless in her approach to life.

My dad, on the other hand, spent all his time working hard at a tyre factory, managing tough bosses and difficult labour problems. He returned home covered in soot and oil. He also worked many night shifts which meant that I hardly saw him. Dad suffered back problems and the strenuous conditions at work strained it further. He had strong views on the status of women in marriage and desired a more submissive wife who not only took care of his needs but also obeyed him.

The contrast between my mum's and my dad's personalities was evident in their conversations. They are people who never shy away from a good fight. Given all this, my parents

---

[43]Pew Research Centre. *ibid.*

are the most loving souls when it comes to me. Their ability to transform from arguing partners to adoring parents instantly made my childhood safe and secure. At the same time, seeing my mum tend and bend, and hearing my dad demand and command made me averse to traditional gender norms of a woman's role at home. I felt compelled to stand up and speak up for equality.

I used to argue vehemently with my dad when I heard him say things like, "A woman must obey her husband," or when he continued to ask my mum to do things for him, after she had wound up for the day. Picture a feisty, assertive girl who knew what she wanted and wasn't afraid of expressing herself. That was me. My brother even sarcastically wished my then husband-to-be, "good luck" before we wed because soon he would have to "manage me". That was my reputation.

Academically, I topped my class in undergraduate and postgraduate and was selected to join one of the top technology companies through campus recruitment at 23. I had barely worked for three months when my parents thought it was high time I got married.

I had an arranged marriage. My parents played a big role in every significant decision, from who to marry to where to marry to what happens at the wedding. I remember refusing to wear a sari when my husband-to-be came to see me with his parents. My mother was satisfied that I wore Indian attire instead of denim pants that day. When my husband-to-be met me for the first time, I told him that I didn't like cooking, wasn't particular about keeping the house clean and was only god-fearing, not religious. I thought it was best to express myself honestly to avoid misgivings on his end.

He went home after that, declaring he wanted to marry me. That decision was quickly conveyed to my mother, and she expected me to jump at the offer. She was so annoyed by my response, I needed time to consider and if she hurried me I would say "no" to the proposal. My mum worked behind my back with her prospective son-in-law to convince me to say "yes". Although uncertain, I eventually fell in love with the persistent man who was sure we were a great match.

Until my wedding, my views on equality were about a man and a woman taking equal responsibility at home. I thought I was an activist for thinking like this. And then, the strangest thing happened after I got married. I switched from this "I Don't do what I Don't want to do" girl to a highly responsible woman, who obsessed with every corner of her home being clean and every meal being perfect.

That switch happened because of fearing judgement by those close to me.

The Conditioning Traps

To achieve being a successful professional, and an excellent homemaker, I developed a two-pronged strategy - to limit my workday as well as restrict what I did during work hours. This meant that I always had an alarm set to 6 pm and a filter in my head to sieve out everything that was not part of my job as per my definition, which included having lunch with my colleagues, coffee chats with peers, and getting to know my colleagues.

My husband's approach to domestic chores was quite different. He went with a "delegate and Don't bother" approach. He insisted that we hire domestic helpers for cooking and cleaning so that neither of us had to bother about these things. He was a supportive spouse and didn't expect me to perform all of the house work.

For crying out loud, what about inventory management, meal planning, doing the work when helpers Don't turn up, managing the helpers, and ensuring work gets done on time and in good quality? "How are we going to get all these done?," should have been my question then, but that never occurred to me as I was so grateful that my husband didn't expect me to cook. When people are grateful, they go to great lengths to reciprocate favourably, and that's what I did.

Remember my two-pronged strategy? The alarm and filter system in my head went through stress testing every day as I tried hard to straddle submission with ambition. It got to a point where I had chosen to relegate my career second to my husband. The good part of this relegation was the ease of relocation. While I hesitated to put my hand up for work opportunities, my husband kept putting up his hand, and we moved almost every two years.

I was expected to follow my husband and move with his career. Therefore, neither my parents nor in-laws commented or questioned it. I was simply following the social norm of being a trailing spouse. My husband didn't even wonder what would happen to my job if he moved. He wasn't being unfair because he was following what he was conditioned to.

My story isn't rare. Across 61 countries surveyed from 2013 to 2019, India came second only to Tunisia, with 55% agreeing with the statement, "When jobs are scarce, men should have more rights to a job than women"[44]. It is common in India for mothers and mothers-in-law to say, "women have to give in for a successful marriage".

Ignorance Isn't Bliss

We moved four times within India and twice internationally. As a trailing spouse, I just asked to be transferred to the same city without worrying about the impact on my career. I embraced every new role wherever I went and was recognised for delighting my clients, as I loved my job as long as it was within my self-imposed limits.

Things went south after I had my baby. That's when I added one more feather to my cap: being my child's primary carer. My child came after ten years of marriage in 2010. I became a mum after so much waiting. I wanted to be part of every aspect of my daughter's life. That's a natural feeling, right? It sure felt like the right approach then.

My husband's job moved again when our child was only ten months old. As always, I asked to be transferred, which was to Singapore this time. My boss was my mentor; she trusted my abilities and wanted me to take on more. She saw the move as

---

[44]Pew Research Centre. *ibid.*

an excellent opportunity for me to increase my visibility, and that's when my career took a sharp turn.

I took up a regional business lead role for my function. Up until then, I had performed a delivery function for 12 years. Working on targets, funnels, proposals, and pitches was new to me.

My alarm and filter system became a pain. The limits I had imposed on my work schedule were severely impacting the pace of learning required to excel in the role, yet I wasn't willing to rethink.

I had gotten so used to being the sole COO and primary carer at home. I was taking on all the load even when we had no domestic help and even when I was not well. I thrived on praise like, "Only you can do this for me, mummy," from my child instead of questioning why that was the case. I grew angry and defensive when anything was pointed out as amiss or a mess. My husband occasionally helped at home, but only when I asked for it or, should I say, screamed for it.

In 2013, I resigned, as my company didn't have a working-from-home or part-time work policy. I discussed the decision with my husband, and we thought it was the best thing to do. My mentor and colleagues were shocked. I'd been promoted that year and was awarded "best consultant" in my group. But the pressure I had put on myself to be the hero at home had gone beyond my tolerance. This was the same year my manager had asked me to travel for business and I was experiencing severe health problems too.

Together We Can

In 2014, my husband and I trained to be a meditation facilitator. Facilitating programmes together helped us relate like colleagues, allowing him to appreciate my strengths. But I still found myself defensive when anything was pointed out as a miss or mess and he continued to offer help only when I asked for it.

The real shift happened only after I became a coach. That's when I started exploring discomfort rather than ignoring it. In addition to that, being part of women's networks helped me to rise above my conditioning.

It took several tough conversations to dig into what had happened and an honest recognition by my husband that there had been significant inequity in the discharge of responsibilities that "bringing home the dough" alone couldn't make up for. His acknowledgment and change enabled me to let go of inhibitions I had harboured for years, wondering if I was doing enough for the family.

I now truly enjoy every role I play without being bothered by others' opinions. What I value most is equilibrium (a state of inner harmony), and decoding discomfort is part of the process.

From my introspective and retrospective lens, here are two steps for you:

1. Be curious about discomfort – When you find yourself angry, frustrated, or defensive doing what you believe

is your choice, ponder if it could be the result of conditioning.

2. Be courageous to recondition yourself – Once you have understood yourself better, speak to those who care about you to help you make choices that align with who you are and what you want.

Equity starts with asking yourself, "What do I need to be successful in my life?"

ABOUT THE AUTHOR

ANUPAMA MURALI

Anupama Murali is an ICF certified Life and Executive Coach, a Certified Neuro Change Method practitioner, Professional Speaker and Leadership Trainer. As the co-founder of Enoughness Mindset coaching programmes, she specialises in enabling highly accomplished individuals to overcome the imposter phenomenon. She is also a senior trainer at MetaMind Training, Singapore's leading leadership training company.

Anupama has over 15 years of global technology consulting experience in multiple roles across Asia, Europe, and North America. She is also a meditation trainer for the last ten years, having conducted over 150 workshops in Singapore.

She became excited about an "inside-out" approach to life when she discovered that she is dynamic yet relaxed when she is in her "Equilibrium", which she defines as a state of inner harmony. Her life's mission now is to empower people to find their "Equilibrium" through her coaching, training and speaking engagements.

You can connect with Anupama at:

Speaker profile on KeyNoteWomen.com:
https://keynotewomen.com/speaker/anupama-murali

: https://www.linkedin.com/in/anupamamurali/

: https://www.anupamamurali.com

STORY TWELVE

The Perils of Privilege

Equity is multi-dimensional

You Don't Miss What You Do Not Have

The last time I visited Kanpur was 13 years ago. I was on maternity leave and wondered how my life would have been had I not moved out. My mother was an ambitious woman who had big dreams for her children. One of her dreams for me was to move out of our sleepy little town and explore the world.

Kanpur is a busy industrial town in North India. It is neither modern nor beautiful, yet worthy enough to make beautiful memories with friends and families. It is the place where I grew up.

Life would surely be different. For better or worse; I do not want to know. I would have missed the richness of experience my geographical mobility has graced me with. I am unsure of what else I would miss; after all, "You Don't miss what you Don't have," so let us fast forward to 2020.

At the peak of the Global Pandemic, I served as the Regional Human Resources Business Partner for one of the world's largest chemical companies. As part of the leadership team, I was nominated to participate in a leadership programmes customised for female leaders. Every session evoked mini transformations within me. One takeaway from the leadership programme that has stayed with me is "privilege is not seen by those who have it".

Over the past two decades, I realised that the most significant peril of privilege is that most of us speak about our privileges, but we do not feel our privilege. In my more than 20 years of corporate experience, I learnt that action is born from feelings, not speaking.

Leaders and managers who have made a positive impact in the corporate world are the ones who felt passionately for a cause rather than the ones who spoke passionately about the cause. The global debate on gender diversity, inclusion and equity would be at a different level if more people felt their privilege.

Speaking about a cause is essential and the first step to generating awareness. However, it seldom evokes transformation. On the other hand, feeling your emotions or privilege can be liberating and can clear internal blockages and mindsets created by our cultural-socio-economic-political background. Daniel Goleman, American psychologist, science journalist and author of the 1995 best seller Emotional Intelligence, states that "true compassion is not only feeling others' pain but also being moved to help relieve it". This "being moved" is where equity stems from.

This brings me to the million-dollar question, why Don't more people feel passionate about things? A lack of passion comes from living a life filled with unsustainable habits and a lack of gratitude. In other words, it's difficult to find passion when constantly wishing to receive and accept more than giving and sharing.

In a situation where we're forever receiving more than we give, we become selfish and that is when we gradually cease feeling for others. Simply put, when we do not feel for others, we are not moved enough to make them feel better and improve their situation. This is also the place where irrelevance stems from. We remain relevant when we put a cap on how much we think about ourselves and start thinking about the communities we belong to.

Privilege is not Seen by Those Who Have it

Cherrie Atilano was born in Silay City, Negros Occidental, Philippines, into a family of sugarcane farmers. She lost her father at three and was raised by a supportive mother and loving family. Cherrie told me about her childhood home and shared stories about how her mum often cooked extra food to share with the neighbours.

One day, 12-year-old Cherrie asked her mother why they often needed to share food with the neighbours. Cherrie's mother put her middle finger on Cherrie's left temple, placed the thumb above Cherrie's chest near her heart and said, "This, my dear, is the shortest distance you need to travel to connect your heart to your brain. If you can't connect these two and all the five senses in between, you will never be able to connect anything in life".

Her mum explained to a young Cherrie that her family had eggplant and shrimp paste to put on the rice for dinner that night, while the neighbours only had boiled rice. This conversation moved Cherrie so much that she started teaching the neighbours how to grow their own vegetables like okra, eggplant and tomatoes.

This was a 12-year-old girl's understanding of equity and the perils of privilege that even after spending significant time with people around us, we often Don't feel their pain. Because we are unaware of the other person's feelings, we are not moved enough to help relieve their pain.

Cherrie is an example of how a woman created and embraced equity in the Farming and Agriculture Industry, which is male-dominated in the Philippines, like most parts of the world. Embracing equity became her recipe for a successful, inspirational entrepreneurial journey.

Her 24 years as a social entrepreneur have been challenging. She says her days are exhausting; however, her life is fulfilling. I do not know of too many people whose passion, purpose and personality are in such unity. Cherrie's fulfilment comes from the harmony in her passion for agriculture, her purpose of serving the poorest of the poor and her charismatic personality because she aims to make farming "sexy" and "desirable".

The Secret Ingredient

Cherrie's passion for agriculture has resulted in the establishment of AGREA, an agriculture business school focusing on supporting and empowering women farmers. Cherrie proposes that if women are the ones securing the food on the table and ensuring the family gets nutrition within a limited budget, then they must be knowledgeable about how food is grown and all the channels through which it travels before it reaches the kitchen and finally the table.

AGREA exposed Cherrie to another peril of privilege that providing women with education was not enough. She soon realised that education alone was not the answer to the problems of the women she was trying to support. These women had to start growing their food to make the effort sustainable. No amount of education will help if a woman is constantly worrying about how to get the next meal on the table. She will not be in the frame of mind to dream big for herself and her family.

Because of this realisation, AGREA taught the theory of growing crops and how to plant seeds practically and nurture crops. More importantly, it taught these willing and able women how to sell the extra produce and become financially independent. AGREA quickly introduced the secret ingredient of "Dreaming" as a part of the curriculum, which included preparing vision boards for these women farmers. This monetary saving and visioning exercise gave the women the courage to dream of a better future.

Life's ways are strange, and our circumstances can sometimes diminish our passion. This is where our life purpose comes in handy to help us to refocus. Cherrie says her greatest gift is that she identified her purpose very early in life. She was 12 years old when she started helping people in her community to grow their own food.

Every time she heard of a farmer in her community committing suicide and the innumerable incidents of domestic violence, she knew she had to help the small-holding farmers to lead dignified lives. This meant a life that included food, enough money to send the children to school and the mental space to dream a better life.

AGREA's mission and success directly contribute to five of the 17 United Nations Sustainable Development Goals – No Poverty, Zero Hunger, Good Health and Well-Being, Quality Education and Gender Equality. It teaches its female students how to grow food, become financially independent, and dream big. The cherry on the cake is that today more than 200 women farmers, some of whom have no formal education and have suffered domestic violence, have bank accounts, nutritious food and school-going children.

Being Relevant

Cherrie is a confident woman who invests in herself and transmits her confidence into her passion, purpose, personality and agriculture. She travels the world advocating for young adults and women and making agriculture a "sexy" and "desirable" profession. It is only natural that multiple Governments and organisations worldwide have awarded her. Being a High-Level Ambassador of the United Nations, Scaling up Nutrition and being awarded the 2020 class of the Young Global Leaders – the World Economic Forum's foundation for remarkable leaders under 40 – are few of the many feathers in her cap. These are privileges that Cherrie was not born with. She created and demanded equity for herself and other women in the male-dominated Agriculture Industry.

Once an entrepreneur has succeeded, it is easy to fall prey to another peril of privilege, the risk of not being relevant, the most dangerous peril of all. To avoid this, Cherrie lives with farmers for weeks and months at a stretch, understanding their daily routines and supporting them with sustainable food systems to increase their monthly family income from farming. With her support, many farming families have raised their monthly income from $60 to $300. It is essential to know that equity is not only an economic equaliser. Equity comes in different forms and shapes. I believe true equity is when every woman in every society and every profession feels a sense of gratitude without compromising her dreams and feels abundant while feeling secure and supported.

Cherrie is one example; our world has many less celebrated and inspiring stars paving the way to a more equitable world. Politicians, corporate leaders, entrepreneurs, working professionals and self-employed individuals from different walks of life are trying to positively impact their communities and workplaces by generating employment, engaging with citizens and employees, ensuring fair practices, leveraging diversity, promoting inclusion and embracing equity. It's a combination of all these and many more spoken and unspoken behaviours that will help us genuinely embody the workplace of the future – an equitable future.

Here are a few statistics to highlight the urgent need for action. According to the World Economic Forum's *Global Gender Gap Report 2022,* in 2021, women accounted for 49.7% of the global population, yet it will still take 132 years for them to reach parity with men[45].

---

[45]World Economic Forum. (2022). *Global Gender Gap Report 2022.* http://reports.weforum.org/global-gender-gap-report-2022 (accessed February 1, 2023).

Connecting Our Heart and Mind

As an HR professional, I know organisations still have a long way to go. Many leaders and managers still speak passionately but do not feel passionate about embracing equity. Few leaders I have worked with speak passionately about building a female talent pipeline but miss the opportunities to connect their intention to the hiring and retention strategy of the organisation.

Another common disconnect I have observed is the need for meaningful questions in exit interviews of female talents. An exit interview that only captures that the female talent is leaving for "better prospects" is a classic example of an exit interview that does not deep dive into questions like "if the female talent felt supported during difficult times". Below is a list of common symptoms that reflect an inequitable workplace:

- Job descriptions that Don't encourage women to apply.
- Under-representation of females in leadership roles.
- Lack of flexible work time.
- Lack of virtual and remote working options.
- Lack of amenities for nursing mothers.
- Succession plans which have fewer female candidates.
- Lack of female superstars in the organisation.
- Fewer stories of successful job rotations of female talents.
- High attrition of female talents.

- Absence of meaningful exit interviews.
- Resolved and unresolved cases of harassment.
- Absence of mentors and coaches for female talents.
- Pay discrimination.
- Low engagement levels.
- Overworked and under-rewarded female colleagues.
- Lack of training budgets for female employees.
- Lack of basic training like unconscious bias and allyship training.
- Instances of microaggression.
- No KPIs and no gender equality targets.

According to the Women at Workplace 2022 report by LeanIn and McKinsey, in Corporate America, one of the top three reasons for women leaders to change jobs is a need for more Diversity, Inclusion and Equity commitment in the organisation. The same report mentions that 31% of senior women leaders and 41% of young women under 30 rank Diversity, Inclusion and Equity as one of the top three important and desired focus areas in an organisation[46].

Equity is multi-dimensional. It fundamentally includes providing equal opportunities to women, encouraging them to apply, setting them up for success, ensuring that the workplace is conducive for them to perform and above all,

---

[46]LeanIn.Org and McKinsey & Company. (2022). *Women in the Workplace 2022.* https://womenintheworkplace.com (accessed February 1, 2023).

allowing women to lead like women. Championing women with non-traditional leadership styles and accepting female energy in boardrooms is a giant leap towards equity.

After speaking to many female professionals, I realised that until the Global Pandemic disrupted our world, the most critical dimension of equity that women were demanding was equal pay, equal opportunities and minimising unconscious biases. However, in the post-pandemic world, women quickly leave organisations that do not provide hybrid or remote working options.

This brings us to the newest peril of privilege, which is providing virtual and remote working options but suffering from flexibility stigma. Flexibility stigma is a recent unfortunate and unfair opinion that women who work flexible hours and work from home are less productive and less committed. Women opting for work-from-home work hard to prove they are as productive and committed as employees who work 9 am to 5 pm in the office.

A shared key to all the above inequity symptoms is having well-trained leaders. When leaders show up consistently, women and organisations benefit. It is, therefore, imperative to equip and reward good leaders. Well-informed and authentic leaders make the right decisions, making women feel treated fairly and less likely to change jobs and leave their careers. If leaders are the key to equity in the workplace, let us look at how we can support them in this journey:

1. Make leaders understand that they are accountable for creating and delivering equity.

2. Set annual targets and periodic milestones that promote equity for all.
3. Acknowledge their attempt to make unbiased hiring.
4. Incentivise them to create equal opportunities for promotions.
5. Provide training courses and periodic refreshers on topics like Diversity, Inclusion and Equity, unconscious bias and allyship training.
6. Train leaders to be a coach and a mentor for female talents.

In conclusion, we are part of an uprising. The Pandemic has disrupted our world like never before. May our generation be remembered for surviving the COVID-19 pandemic and for supportive mothers who taught their children the first lesson in embracing equity.

May we be remembered for our female professionals who dared to move out of sleepy towns, encouraged other women to dream of a better life, and as the generation that "felt their privilege" and was "moved to take steps" to make our world more equitable. An equitable world where all men and women, young and old, managers and subordinates, leaders and followers, governments and citizens are coming together to shape the future of work. Let's shape this well.

ABOUT THE AUTHOR

SURABHI KAPOOR

Surabhi Kapoor was born in India to parents who valued education and fairness. Growing up with an elder brother, she felt loved and empowered to make the choices her heart desired and was also supported by her family to succeed in every decision she made. She sees this as a privilege because many of her girlfriends were raised differently. This childhood privilege and her workplace challenges of attracting and retaining female talent laid the foundation for her being an advocate for gender diversity, inclusion and equity.

Surabhi has a Master's in Business Administration, and she is a certified Coach and a yoga practitioner. She has more than 20 years of international and leadership experience in the field of Human Resources.

She also invests significant time volunteering for not-for-profit organisations like WOMAG and the KeyNote Women Speaker Directory.

She currently works and lives in Dubai with her partner and two children.

You can connect with Surabhi at:

✉ : surabhikapoor@gmail.com

in : https://www.linkedin.com/in/surabhi-kapoor/

STORY THIRTEEN

In Case of Doubt: Promote Her

Mothers are some of the best employees you can wish for.

February 2018

I'm closing my laptop. Time to head to the airport for my flight. On my way out, I ran into the partner I work with. Let's call him Anders*.

"Thanks for your help in today's session. I'm leaving for my flight home. I'll finish the document tonight," I tell him.

"Great workshop Anna. Next time bring those other colours sticky notes," he answers.

Anders is the partner I work with most. He is the Asia practice lead for our people strategy work, which is my area of expertise. Pretty much all the work I do involves collaborating with him.

Anders' standard is extreme. He is never satisfied. No matter how great your work is, he will remind you that something could have been done better. He keeps you on your toes and pushes you higher. It's become exhausting.

"Have you heard from Aaron yet?" he asks as I reach for the door.

Aaron is my evaluator, an Associate Partner from New York. I'm up for promotion, and Associate Partner is the next level. It's been four years since my last promotion. An eternity in management consulting, where a promotion every two years means your career is "on track". Sure, the role switch and leaves of absence didn't help, but four years is still a long time. Some analysts on my team received their promotions so fast they would soon be ahead of me.

"Not yet. The evaluation committee had their session yesterday. Aaron is supposed to call me today with the outcome. He told me he'll try to catch me on my way to the airport".

"Message me once you hear the good news. You deserve this one. It should be in the pocket". The regional leadership was fully supportive.

I believe in meritocracy: Being overdue for a promotion doesn't entitle you to get it. Promotions are earned. Delivering results. Or maybe they planted this in my head: Whenever the review was disappointing, it felt like it was me. I hadn't worked hard enough. I hadn't ticked all the boxes.

That is why this time around, I felt good about my chances. This time around, I did tick all the boxes. I had gone above and beyond. Brought in a new client, grew an existing account, and introduced a new offering. Over the past year, I flew all over the region, facilitated client workshops in Shanghai and Tokyo and was a good "citizen of the firm" by taking the lead for internal activities.

Heck, I even squeezed my private life into the mould as much as I could. I will never forget going through fertility treatment and injecting myself with hormones in an aeroplane toilet 30,000 ft in the sky to join an urgent client meeting.

I didn't cut corners. Not even when, in my first trimester, morning sickness turned out to be an all-day event. I was so sick that after arriving at my client's office in Penang, I had to take the first flight back to Singapore, followed by three weeks in bed, too nauseous even to scroll my phone but taking calls to ensure my "client came first".

And so today, if all went well, Aaron would give me good news, and I would finally see the reward for this hard work.

Tons of research has shown what we knew all along: having a gender-diverse senior leadership team delivers real value to the business[47]. Our global economy leaves trillions of dollars on the table due to the lack of gender equality in work and society[48]. Women are hugely underrepresented at the senior leadership level.

In their careers, women face undercurrents that no white men have to deal with. The world is designed for men, and women are a niche[49].

The hurdles women face to thrive in a world designed for men and to reach the top start early in their careers. Women make up 50% of entry-level positions[50]. They are ambitious: From the cohort of women aged 18-44, 15% want to be C-suite level within ten years[51]. Yet, for every 100 entry-level men promoted to manager, only 87 of their women peers are promoted.

---

[47]McKinsey & Company. (2020). *Diversity Wins: How Inclusion Matters.*

[48]McKinsey & Company. (2015). *The Power of Parity: How Advancing Women's Equality Can Add $12 Trillion To Global Growth.*

[49]Criado-Perez, C. (2019). *Invisible Women: Exposing Data Bias in a World Designed for Men.* Abrams Press.

[50]McKinsey & Company. (2019). *Women in the Workplace.*

[51]CNBC and Survey Monkey. (2020). *Women at Work.*

We never catch up. So, we leave. Despite many efforts to change this, we are losing high-potential women leaders with the floodgates open. They call it The Great Breakup. Women leave to change jobs, change companies, change careers. It needs to stop.

Women Don't leave because of family reasons. They leave their jobs because of workplace conditions. They leave because of a lack of opportunity to advance, a lack of support, a lack of flexibility and a lack of an organisation's commitment to Diversity, Equity and Inclusion (DEI)[52].

March 2018

"He stabbed me in the back. After everything I've done for him, he stabbed me in the back. I've been nothing but good. I even flew him into Kuala Lumpur (KL) to join the client workshop".

I'm ranting to Daniel, our product manager from New York is visiting me in Singapore. He is joining me for client visits and a big client event. Tonight we're having a well-deserved after-work drink.

And as the topic comes up, we discuss why I didn't get that promotion. Out of seven upward reviews from the analysts I had been working with, six were raving and said things like "Anna is my role model" or "Anna is the leader I want to work with". But one review was different. And although the reviews are anonymous, I knew who this came from and why.

---

[52]McKinsey & Company. (2022). *Women in the Workplace.*

For the telco client Anders and I served, I had been working with Dipesh. Unhappy in his role as an analyst and keen to transfer to Canada, he became bitter when his transfer fell through. Leaving the firm was his only option to join his wife in Canada.

In his last months, he took it out on others. He was hard to work with. The quality of his work went down, and that bothered Anders. I was stuck in the middle. How to motivate someone who was leaving anyway?

On one occasion, as we were preparing for one of the workshops, I decided to step out of the middle and let them sort it out. That backfired. It was clear in the upward feedback: "Anna doesn't protect her team; she throws them to the wolves". Naïve as I was, I thought the committee would understand the context. But they didn't.

"So, not only did I not get my promotion, but I'm also now seen as "not a people leader", despite these six rave reviews telling them I'm exactly the people leader colleagues want to work with".

Daniel lets me rant.

"I can only imagine how frustrating this must be. Travelling with you this week, I see how much effort you put in," Daniel says. "If our team in the US would put in this much effort, we'd triple our revenue. You're doing fantastic work".

Fantastic work or not, I didn't get my promotion. I'm due in August. During the next promotion cycle, I'll be on maternity leave. I have only five months to get that two-years-overdue promotion. "How will I do in five months what I wasn't able to do in 12 months?" I ask myself.

Women are held to different standards. Compared to men, 94% of women in tech feel that more is expected from them at work, and 86% of women in tech have been accused of being too emotional in the workplace[53]. In performance reviews, women are called "bossy, abrasive, strident, aggressive, irrational and emotional"[54].

Motherhood provides women with a double whammy. Women get a 4% cut in pay for every child they have, whereas men, on average, get a 6% increase[55]. Working mums and dads agree that women are penalised in their careers for starting a family, while men are not. Most working Americans believe that working mums are more likely to be passed up for a new job and that career opportunities are given to less qualified employees instead of working moms who may be more skilled[56].

There's also unconscious bias towards mothers. Managers often subconsciously make assumptions about what is best

---

[53]Navisite. (2022). *The Gender Divide in Tech.*

[54]Criado-Perez, C. (2019). *Invisible Women: Exposing Data Bias in a World Designed for Men.* Abrams Press.

[55]Budig, M. (2014). *The Fatherhood Bonus and the Motherhood Penalty: Parenthood and the Gender Gap in Pay.* https://www.thirdway.org/report/the-fatherhood-bonus-and-the-motherhood-penalty-parenthood-and-the-gender-gap-in-pay (accessed February 15, 2023).

[56]Bright Horizons (2018). *Bright Horizons Modern Family Index.* https://www.brighthorizons.com/-/media/bh-new/newsroom/media-kit/mfi_2018_report_final.ashx (accessed February 14, 2023).

for a mother and her career, sending her home early to care for children, passing on her for a role that might add too much workload, or finding someone else to travel overseas for an important client visit. These micro-moves have a butterfly effect on women's career advancement.

September 2018

I was on maternity leave. In late August, I gave birth to our first child. It was quite the whirlwind a few weeks before that: My client relationships were gone because elections had reshuffled leadership in government-linked companies; I travelled to 8 different countries, some multiple times; and I pitched our offerings to 100s of CEOs and CFOs at various events. One week before giving birth, I pitched in Kuala Lumpur to the leadership of a Fortune 500 company. Two days later, I pitched in Singapore to the Head of People of a large local bank. Both projects were confirmed shortly after I gave birth.

Juggling how to take on this new identity as a mother, I enlarged my circle with new "mummy-friends". At one time, I was invited to the inner circle of colleagues: mums, soon-to-be-mums and wannabe-mums. It was my first social interaction with colleagues since I became a mother, and here I was for an intimate Sunday brunch.

"Have you heard the latest?" asked my colleague who was pregnant with twins. "Seriously, you're not going to believe this!" she added before anyone could answer.

"Believe what?" someone replied.

"The Firm now allows you to FedEx your breastmilk home. How awesome! You can pump in the hotel and send it home so your nanny can feed your baby". I looked at my daughter, sleeping in the car seat on the floor next to me. FedEx-ing my breastmilk home. I will have two more months of paid maternity leave, and then they will pay to FedEx my breastmilk home.

To stand out in a field of highly skilled colleagues, you need luck. The Paradox of Skill tells us that in situations where skill and luck play a role in determining the outcome, luck becomes more important when overall competence levels increase.[57] Imagine working for one of the world's most pre-eminent management consulting firms with the smartest graduates from the world's top universities. The absolute skill level is incredibly high. To stand out, luck plays a huge role.

Looking forward, we can see how luck will play a role in how our life pans out. But once success is achieved, our brain develops the narrative that it happened because of our skills and tricks us into believing that that narrative is the only possible narrative. We fail to see how lucky we may have been. The right client at the right time.

This is why leaders today struggle to "think outside the box" when solving the gender equality gap. They have become biased, believing that whatever their journey has been should be everyone else's journey as well. They have a template in mind that is hard to deviate from. Women are offered a

---

[57]Talks at Google. (2014). *The Success Equation: Untangling Skill and Luck, Michael Mauboussin.*

career template designed for men. Instead of redesigning it, we make adjustments, like FedEx-ing breastmilk.

Survivor bias leads us to draw conclusions based on a skewed sample set of those who made it. We fail to take into account those who didn't make it. The survivors work long hours, so that must be a primary factor to success, but how many of those who dropped out along the way also worked long hours?

Hindsight and survivor bias are just two of the many biases that get in the way of women's career advancement. The most twisted one is the "I am not biased" bias, something highly intelligent people are most prone to. "Our performance reviews are fair; we are not biased".

The issue is that we fail to recognise the role luck and biases have played in our careers. The problem is that we believe things have been fair. Our striving for fairness gets in the way of true equality. To achieve a world where everyone has equal chances of success, we must let go of our current perception of fairness and embrace equity.

November 2018

"Are you nervous?" my husband asks. "Not really. I mean, I've done what I could. I can't predict it. I Don't know what to expect anymore. It feels random. I just want to get this over with," I answered.

"Anna, how are things? It has been such a joy to do this evaluation," Blake said as I joined the video conference. After February, Blake took over from Aaron as my evaluator, which was an upside. Where Aaron was relatively junior, Blake was seasoned, and she knew the Asian market inside out.

"Congratulations, the committee is so impressed with everything you've been doing, and we're delighted to let you know that you made it to Associate Partner".

My head was spinning. Happy, yes, but sad at the same time. It was all a little too late. "Wow, that is great news, Blake. Thank you", I answered. Two months later, I resigned.

Mothers are some of the best employees you can wish for. Proven by research, mothers are more productive than women without children[58]. Also, they are seen as better listeners, calmer in crisis, more diplomatic and better team players than fathers or childless employees[59].

And having mothers in your workforce has a spill-over effect: 89% of people believe that mothers in leadership roles bring out the best in their employees, and 40% of women are more likely to stay with their current employer for the next five years if their boss is a mother. Two-thirds of women employees say having a manager who is a mother enhances their overall team morale, and 23% say they have an overall more positive workplace experience with a manager who is a mother.[60]

---

[58]Krapf, M. et al., Federal Bank of St. Louis. (2014). *Parenthood and Productivity of Highly Skilled Labor: Evidence from the Groves of Academe.* Science Direct, August 2017. https://www.sciencedirect.com/science/article/abs/pii/S0167268117301397 (accessed February 14, 2023).

[59]Bright Horizons Modern Family Index. (2018).

[60]The Mom Project. (2021). *Moms Are Drivers of Success in the Workplace.*

To all of you leaders: It is time we take a chance on women, specifically mothers. Give them the benefit of the doubt. Hire them, promote them, and fight to keep them. We need these women, and this slow train of half-baked initiatives isn't getting us there. We need to aggressively advance women. Embrace the discomfort of potentially making a mistake and taking a risk to see where they may bring us. Because frankly, how many more good women can we afford to lose?

And to all of you women who see my story as your own: Think about how long you will allow them to dangle this carrot in front of you. You might be close to that promotion, but how much is a sunk cost? As you wait for that promotion, what is your opportunity cost of other options? Which alternative careers would be as good or even better? Because now that I'm on the other side, I can tell you this: there are other ways.

**Names have been changed.*

ABOUT THE AUTHOR

ANNA JOKE BREIMER BHARATI

Anna Joke Breimer Bharati is passionate about leadership development and working with the leaders of the future. Through her brand Tomorrow College she helps leaders develop the power skills they need, and with her Courageous Teams solution, she helps those leaders come together in powerful teams.

Before creating these solutions under her company, The Breimer Group, Anna was an Associate Partner with McKinsey & Company, spending close to a decade with the consulting firm in Europe, the Middle East and Asia. During her time as a consultant, Anna specialised in leadership, people analytics, teamwork, and talent.

Originally from The Netherlands and residing in Singapore for over a decade, Anna holds a BSc in Building Sciences, an MSc in Architectural Engineering and an MBA from INSEAD.

Anna has passionately been involved in many initiatives to advance women throughout her career. These range from recruiting to specialised training programmes, research projects, mentorship and dedicated events.

You can connect with Anna at:

: https://www.linkedin.com/in/anna-joke-breimer-bharati/

: https://www.courageousteams.com/

: https://www.tomorrow.college/

STORY FOURTEEN

The Equity-Driven Marriage

Relationships need attention, time, effort and commitment

Relationship equity in a marriage is a tough balancing act to follow, more so to achieve. In contrast to equity in a friendship, workplace or community, which may only involve balance, fairness and impartiality, relationship equity in a healthy, loving relationship requires much more.

Equity allows for some level of individualism where the individuals' needs are emphasised, while the WE aspect will also have to be considered in relationship equity. *Relationship Equity in a marriage is when both spouses have the power to make choices for their individual selves and the ability to take action in a way that feels fair and balanced for their WE.*

Finding the balance, where all needs of the I and the WE are met, makes for an ideal situation with a healthy give and take. What should this balance look like? The balance will also have to consider other important ingredients in a marriage, such as love and connection, bringing out the best in each other, sharing enjoyable moments, creating and achieving life goals, and finding meaning and purpose in a shared life.

Try to achieve all of that while striving for equity as well. Is it possible to balance all of that and still have equity? Are we aspiring for something that doesn't exist? If we aspire to a perfect balance, we are in for disappointment. As the shared journey unravels, an evolving balance across the lifespan is more realistic.

In my work with expatriate couples as a Counselling Psychologist and a Relationship Therapist, I have encountered quite a few cases of relationships that are challenged with finding the equity they need. A specific situation to illustrate this is the experience of a "trailing spouse" who moves to cities or countries because of a job their spouse has taken, leaving most of them with no purpose and aimlessly following wherever the job may take them. The story usually starts with "I am just a trailing spouse", a statement that I have heard in my office, with resignation or resentment, for over two decades.

They continue to describe how they intentionally need to find a way to make the situation work for them by filling up their days with what their host country can offer, whether that's part of their life purpose or not. Since your husband asked if we should do this, you said yes, thinking this is the right thing to do while putting your needs aside. You just have to make it work.

Being an expatriate wife myself, it is a question that I have also been asked with curiosity and tentativeness in the last 25 years. The term "trailing" is defined by someone following behind, moving slowly and wearily. It is an experience shared in many different ways by women who have found themselves stuck in the expatriate bubble of their husbands' highly successful careers. They feel the lack of equity in many ways and yet move on as best as they can.

I have encouraged the women I counsel to use the term "travelling spouse" instead. This newer label connotes a sense of togetherness, a shared journey and a team effort to accomplish goals that they have chosen together. It recognises that both partners can and should contribute in many ways that allow them to grow as two individuals and as a committed WE. This becomes especially important when the couples also have children to raise as their family grows in their new situation.

Helen felt inferior in her marriage. She and her husband have been married for 22 years and have moved five times. She met her husband in Canada, where she was born and raised, while he was on a work assignment from Germany, where he is originally from. They are now on their fifth job posting in Singapore. Her husband liked to emphasise that he was alone in providing for the family in private and in public, usually leaving Helen embarrassed.

He says he feels miserable with little time to do the things he enjoys. He resented Helen's hobbies and social events while he was stuck in meetings and calls. Why couldn't she find a job just like his mother, who had a career until retirement? He constantly asked her to send out resumes and find a "proper" job to pay the bills stating that women can have successful careers too. Why not her?

He constantly chided her for spending time in the gym, playing tennis, or attending ladies' lunches. "What a 'good life' you have," he says. Since the kids were leaving the nest, he wanted to return to Europe and take a break. He adds, "It is now her turn to find a job and work at his level".

Their relationship was not always like this. There were so many good things that brought them together. He was smart and funny, and they shared many things. He built her confidence to pursue many things. How could things change so drastically? Our sessions made her realise that he was going through a transition as well that was triggering memories from his childhood where money was difficult, his father left them, and he had to work at such an early age to help his mother through all of that.

Helen was confused and distressed that after leaving her career, which back in the days had so much potential, to follow her husband and achieve his career progression in several countries. Now he expected her to pick up her old job just like that, even though she had not worked for the last 20 years. Who would hire her now, after being out of circulation in the professional field for this long?

Research shows us that, "*Common interests may lead one or both partners to expect or feel obligated to give a lower priority to their individual career interests in order to invest in the 'collective project called family' .... In general, women experience less continuity in the life domain of work because of their responsibility for dependent lives*"[61].

This common situation described above can branch out into many versions and aspects of it that represent the lack of equity in marriage. The trailing spouse has no choice, giving up all they have built to follow their spouse while feeling diminished and minimised for not achieving enough or doing something worthwhile.

Robyn has been a trailing spouse for 12 years since leaving Spain, her home country. She had met her husband in a

---

[61]van der Klis, M. and Mulder, C.H. (February 9, 2008). "Beyond the trailing spouse: the commuter partnership as an alternative to family migration" *Journal of Housing and Built Environment. (23): 1-9.*

month-long training course in the United States, where he is originally from. They have now moved three times with two very young children. The pandemic made her realise that she wants to be back in Spain, where the lifestyle is freer and more expansive and offers a variety of activities because of its outdoor terrain.

She missed home, and it was time to head back. Can she decide this on her own, or would this mean the end of her marriage? Culturally she wanted to be back with her "tribe" where there was familiarity, acceptance and comfort. Her husband continued to have a contract he had to fulfil for another two years, and she is not sure if she can wait that long.

His career had always been the priority. Does it have to continue that way? Her thoughts revolve around "I Don't contribute much as I am not earning" and "my needs are not as important as he has the 'big job'". She adds, "His career is more important, and so we make decisions based on it". So, we went where it took us.

He quickly immersed himself in the workplace structure while she set up "home", identifying where all that made up their home, school, church, and community life could be met. At some point, there will be time for herself after the family has adjusted and adapted to the newness of their host country. Will there be space for her career that she left when this is all over? She is tired and wants something for herself. How can one introduce equity when one spouse realises they are unhappy and what she needs will make her husband unhappy? Robyn worries that the only way for her to meet this need is to leave the marriage.

Relationships are strained because of experiences like Helen's and Robyn's. It's like a competition most couples share. Complaints naturally follow, like "I Don't get enough sleep. I Don't get to buy the things I want. I do most of the chores around the house. I Don't get as much time with friends. My hobbies and interests are not as valued. My dreams, hopes and plans are not given as much attention. What about me, and what I want?" These questions can signal the beginning of resentment.

This experience has also been shared by men when it happens in reverse and the husband is trailing. It is important to be aware of how equity can be maintained for both spouses in their current life situation.

If either of the couple finds themselves, intentionally or otherwise, hyper-focused on making everything equal, it could likely lead to more compounding problems. Anyone stuck in the pattern of thinking about what they are NOT getting out of their arrangement only traps themselves in building up resentment, contempt and criticism. All the scorekeeping, tit-for-tat, and irritations soon add up and diminish the love and care for each other.

Although my work is with expatriates, I see themes that are relevant for many couples. Research tells us that women are more likely than men to "give more" to the marriage at any given marital duration. Women dismiss the imbalance in relationships because of traditional roles and messages that expect them to stay the "emotional glue" of the family. Knowing this, would equity really be essential for us women in a marriage when messages like these are conveyed through generations? There are other blocks to relationship equity in marriages that are worth mentioning.

Our cultures significantly influence the individual's expectations and perceptions of what a spouse should do in a marriage and for the family. Certain cultural norms have set responsibilities based on gender and role assignments.

There are also gender roles that assign specific tasks to women and men that show up in the dynamics of family life and lifestyle choices. Some women have become resigned to this because this is what traditions impose upon us, and they feel it is impossible to change. Husbands are allowed less time and energy for the family, and women should solely focus on their role as homemakers.

Power and control in a marriage can also take away equity. For example, when one spouse controls access to money, which prevents the other from choosing freely, equity is not present. Controlling through emotional unavailability, like silent treatment, withdrawal, and isolation can make one feel burdened in a relationship. Solo socialising and withholding information can disconnect the couple and take away that sense of equity.

Despite these blocks, I hope we can believe that equity is a necessity for every couple. Knowing that we want what is best for each other to flourish in life with meaning is essential. As partners, we are willing to support that for one another.

Trust that balance will always be the goal. Unique individual differences may tip this balance once in a while, but with effective communication, we find our way back to equity.

Both partners contribute in many valuable ways, allowing them to grow as two individuals and a committed WE. A shared relationship vision can guide us in taking the first step towards that healthy give and take. Our sense of equity may have to be revisited through the long haul. Regularly come together to explore how equity is present in your marriage and make it just right for you.

Studies show inequitable marriages are more likely to dissolve[62]. Thus, Helen's marriage ended two years ago when their children were off to university, and she could not meet the requirement of finding that "proper job". Robyn plans to move back at the end of the year when her husband's contract ends. Robyn was willing to wait, and her husband was willing to understand her world. He decided that he wanted a break, and they had created enough financial security to do this at this time. The children were at an age where they would benefit from some time in their home country. They both re-created a new relationship vision to meet their needs at this stage.

It will take time to create a relationship atmosphere that is equity inspired rather than equality driven. Give each other the benefit of the doubt that equity is what you want. If you

---

[62]DeMaris, A. (June 27, 2010). "The 20-Year Trajectory of Marital Quality in Enduring Marriages: Does Equity Matter?" *J. Soc. Pers. Relat.* (4): 449-471.

have been married for many years, take that first step to create new habits. Watch your relationship switch to a deeper and more meaningful connection. Grow an equity-driven relationship implementing the strategies outlined below:

Embrace the attitude of curiosity about one another.

Express interest in your daily individual lives and how it can influence the WE.

Quality regular dialogue. Or **Q**uit striving for equality.

Regularly communicate about experiences, needs, dreams, and passion.

Avoid keeping score on who does what.

Understand your goals as a couple and family.

Support one another in goals that you would like to achieve.

Introduce daily caring behaviour

Express love and care daily.

Time to recreate new ways of being with each other.

Schedule time with one another in your calendar for recreational and leisurely activities.

Yearly assessment of what needs to start, stop and continue to work to keep equity in the marriage.

Create a relationship vision for the future, knowing your needs today.

Marriage is hard work. Relationships need attention, time

and commitment. It takes two people to make it work. Strive to maintain a peaceful, pleasant, and happy relationship environment by aspiring to embrace equity in your relationship. Make things right for you and each other. When you want to love your spouse, you are willing to stretch out towards many things, including the unfamiliar.

Most women will know what they are willing to do to love. For many women, more so than men, good intimate relationships are central to their well-being. They are willing to give much, much more. Research states, "Women are believed to give more than they receive in relationships, especially with respect to interpersonal resources such as self-disclosure, emotional support, and empathic understanding"[63].

Looking back now, I may have redefined the rules for myself and my career by being a "travelling spouse". It would have been a smaller ocean if I didn't "trail" him. Life may throw surprises our way; the choice to break even or break through is ours. Find ways to make your life's journey work for you as a couple and prepare for the twists and turns of life. With love and commitment to your growth, your spouse's growth and the good of the relationship, equity will flow naturally.

**Names have been changed.*

---

[63]DeMaris, A. *ibid.*

ABOUT THE AUTHOR

LISSY ANN PUNO

Lissy Ann Puno is a Counselling Psychologist and Co-Founder of the International Counselling & Psychology Centre, a leading mental health private practice in Singapore offering counselling and psychotherapy. She has 30 years of experience working in psychological health and emotional well-being in the United States, the Philippines, Malaysia, Thailand and Singapore, where she is a sought-after clinician and speaker.

She is an avid workshop presenter bringing people closer together through the Getting the Love You Want workshop for couples and the Connected Parents, Thriving Kids workshop for parents. As an author, Lissy has launched several books on relationship wellness and creating strong marriages beginning with Affairs Don't Just Happen, Stay Connected and Couple Goals.

Lissy aims to inspire others to maintain meaningful connections with the people in their life, enabling them to navigate the journey with a joyful purpose. She is a "connected-nester" with her husband of 33 years, managing her "commuter family" with two adult children.

You can connect with Lissy at:

Speaker profile on KeyNoteWomen.com:
https://keynotewomen.com/speaker/lissy-puno

: www.intlcounselling.com

:https://www.instagram.com/stayconnectedlissypuno/

STORY FIFTEEN

Removing the Inequity that Impedes Progress

It is humanly impossible to be a superwoman.

Why did I even do a PhD if I was going to quit my science career just two years later? I got my PhD through a lot of sacrifice, hard work and tears. Yet I left research.

I recall my 21-year-old self on a plane from India to New York. I was the first girl from my family and friendship circle to pursue a doctorate with a full scholarship in cell and molecular biology. This was in 2001, and looking back, I applaud my parents for supporting my decision and letting me fly across the seas with a couple of traveller's cheques and change to a foreign land.

I was filled with both nervous excitement and heaviness in my heart. On one hand, I was flying closer to my dream, but on the other, I was flying far away from my people, especially Ashwin, my junior college sweetheart. He was sailing as a second officer in Merchant Marine at that time.

The following year, I made new friends, survived the extreme winter in Buffalo, NY, and went through intensive courses and qualifying exams. In mid-2002, Ashwin and I decided to get married with a conscious choice to prioritise our careers, especially my PhD. Though an extremely tough situation, our relationship, built on love, trust and respect for one another, blossomed into a beautiful one despite the long distance.

After four more years, I obtained my PhD with the Dean's award. At the end of my thesis defence, I broke down as I was sharing my gratitude, moving my audience to tears as many of them were my peers and well-wishers who had witnessed my journey through science closely.

Despite all this, I quit my career in science.

After living by myself for five years in cold, wintry Buffalo, away from people I loved, I wanted a normal life as much as I wanted a successful career. I moved back to India, rejecting the opportunity to pursue research in top institutes in the US, including MIT. I simply wanted to spend time with the man I married and have a "life". I sailed with him for a few months and then took up a research job at a multinational pharmaceutical company based in Bangalore. I loved my new drug discovery job and appreciated the opportunity to see my folks in Kerala more often.

The twist to my story began with a medical diagnosis. I cannot forget the day when the doctor passed the verdict that "you both are not capable of conceiving a child naturally and may try assisted reproductive technology". I could barely sleep that night. God, I thought getting a PhD was tough. Staying away from my people was tough. Now this?

We had no choice but to start taking fertility treatments. We would go in for treatments when Ashwin came home from sailing. Our sweet relationship was tested by the sourness of failed fertility treatments. The only time we had together was spent in clinics and in anticipation of seeing that positive line on the pregnancy test kit.

At one point, I couldn't take it anymore. The lack of my biological productivity, aka reproduction, coupled with my husband's absence most times, had affected my well-being and productivity at work. I couldn't put my heart and soul into anything anymore. I was beginning to give up. One day,

I told Ashwin and my family that I was quitting my job.

I needed to choose life or career. It seemed to me that my life and career were separate paths and that I couldn't have it all. In that moment in time, I had this deep realisation that I was experiencing inequity first hand.

The Prevalence of Inequity

Was *it just me?* As my reason for leaving my career was more than just the common challenges a woman would face when starting a family, I thought it was just me who felt this way. Although I had all the support from my husband, family and employers to pursue my career, what made me feel the need to choose one over the other?

Looking back, I identified three underlying reasons for my exhaustion and emotional drain. First was my belief that I had to give it my all. The moment I felt I could not give 100% to work and life simultaneously, I felt I must quit. Secondly, my physical exhaustion was compounded by mental exhaustion caused by social comparison and seeing others' projects, careers, and lives take off. The question that zapped my energy the most was, "Why me?" Third, I was prey to unconscious social expectations of gender roles determining what I "should" prioritise.

Today, I know it's not just me. As a coach and mentor for women in STEM (Science, Technology, Engineering and Mathematics), I see brilliant women often setting very high expectations of themselves whilst not giving themselves enough credit for their accomplishments. Most women want to give it their all and feel disappointed with themselves when they do not top it all or can't have it all. The dilemma of choosing a career versus life is real for women, and we seldom hear men facing this.

As I write this, I hear the news of New Zealand Prime Minister Jacinda Ardern's resignation. After giving her all to the country for over five years, she has chosen to spend time with her family. I truly respect her decision and admire her self-awareness and strength to make such a bold and courageous decision. But deep inside, I cannot help thinking that women, irrespective of who they are, where they are from, and what power they hold, still have to go through situations in life when they face this predicament of choosing one over the other - life or career.

Falling Victim to Inequity

After I left my job, I focused fully on my fertility treatments in a trusted clinic in my hometown, Kerala. After two years filled with prayers, tears and hope, I conceived and gave birth to our first son. I found happiness all over again.

A year later, we moved to Singapore, where my husband found a shore job, which meant that finally, after ten years of marriage, we got to live under the same roof. After we settled in and I found good childcare options for my son, I yearned to get back to research. However, the career break, relocation and lack of a professional network in Singapore made it very tough for me to land a research job. This was the first consequence of my choice between life and career, an inequitable choice that many women have to make. I realised that I had to pivot, and with much persistence for two years, I got a job in an alternative science career, surprisingly, at a time when I was expecting our second child. I was overwhelmed with joy and felt I finally had everything: family and a job.

Things began to look up initially until unexpected new challenges gripped me. The field of work was new to me, and I began to feel I was not good enough for this role as I learnt that my work was not meeting the expectations of my new workplace. I tried hard to prove myself but failed.

At home, I was drained by the demands of an infant and a four-year-old. I soon reached a point of burnout and was diagnosed with chronic fatigue. As I had taken a pay cut and joined at an entry level out of desperation for a job, I also felt small and insignificant in my organisation. There were so many times when I just wanted to give up. So many moments when I searched in desperation for that energetic, aspirational, bold girl on that plane to New York.

During those times, my solace was the women in the science group within my organisation, which gave me a sense of purpose. Through this group, I learnt that I am not alone in my journey and learnt about the phenomenon of the "Leaky pipe in STEM", where women drop out of STEM careers at a high rate at earlier points in their careers[64].

---

[64]UNESCO. (2015). UNESCO Science Report: Towards 2030. *UNESCO Publishing*. https://unesdoc.unesco.org/ark:/48223/pf0000235406. (accessed February 8, 2023).

Those women who manage to hold on to their careers struggle to move up the career ladder, hitting the glass ceiling. According to the most recent *UNESCO Science Report*[65], in academia, female researchers experience a gender pay gap and shorter careers, and their work is underrepresented in high-profile journals. A recent article in Nature highlights a report by Mothers in Science, a women-led non-profit organisation, on the funding inequity experienced by women researchers and calls for policy changes to eliminate this[66]. In industry, women are underrepresented in leadership roles.

Thus, once we fall victim to inequity, we fall behind in the race. Many women lose the opportunity to either get back into careers or face a point of stagnation, unable to move into senior or leadership roles.

The Price of Inequity

The growing inequity underlies the gender equality seen globally and in STEM fields. As reported by the International Labour Organisation (ILO)[67], the current global labour force participation rate for women is just under 47%, whereas for

---

[65]UNESCO, (2021). UNESCO Science Report: The Race Against Time for Smarter Development. *UNESCO Publishing.* https://www.unesco.org/reports/science/2021/en. (accessed February 8, 2023).

[66]Heidt, A. (January 27, 2023). "A call to create funding equity for researcher-mums". *Nature.* https://www.nature.com/articles/d41586-023-00252-5. (accessed February 8, 2023).

[67]International Labour Organization. (n.d.). *The gender gap in employment: What's holding women back?* https://www.ilo.org/infostories/en-GB/Stories/Employment/barriers-women#intro (accessed February 8, 2023).

men, it's 72%. The reasons vary depending on socioeconomic constraints and pressure to conform to traditional gender roles. In STEM fields, although there has been some progress, it has been uneven, with the average representation of women in STEM less than one-third.

The ultimate price of inequity is losing highly educated and talented women from the STEM workforce, which is not just a personal loss but a significant intellectual and economic loss. I

have come across many driven and talented women in STEM with doctorates trying to get back into the workforce following a career break.

A study conducted by the European Institute for Gender Equality (EIGA) reveals the economic benefits of closing the gender gap for women in STEM. As shown by this research, by 2050, improving gender equality would increase EU (GDP) per capita by 6.1 to 9.6%, which amounts to €1.95 to €3.15 trillion[68].

But are we doing enough to close the gender gap? I have not seen any formal policies or measures to support those women in science whose careers halted or slowed down. Even in other industries, I only see grassroots level, mainly women-led initiatives that are striving to do something about it. While I am glad that there are more efforts to encourage more girls to take up STEM, unless the leak in the career pipe

---

[68]European Institute for Gender Equality. (n.d.). *Economic Benefits of Gender Equality in the European Union.* https://eige.europa.eu/gender-mainstreaming/policy-areas/economic-and-financial-affairs/economic-benefits-gender-equality. accessed February 8, 2023.

is closed to retain those women who enter the workforce, the net gain will be nil as we will still end up losing women from the STEM workforce.

Towards Societal and Economic Progress

The price of inequity is inarguably high. Our planet's future depends on innovative, sustainable measures to address global threats from climate change, growing social divides, poverty, and uneven global recovery from the pandemic. Science and technology are key to finding new solutions for these problems, which depend on the collective intelligence, skills, knowledge and diverse perspectives of the people in STEM. Therefore, eliminating inequity in STEM fields is necessary for progress.

As the cause for inequity is multifactorial and exists at multiple levels, it is important to address it from different angles. Inequity spreads like weeds when left unattended. I propose that inequity be weeded from three levels – *System, Society and Self.*

It is imperative that inequity be removed from the *System* level, where policy, organisational and government-level changes are required to create widespread, permanent changes. Flexible work hours, remote/hybrid work, dedicated nursing rooms at offices, child care leave, mentorship programme, coaching and training support, government initiatives to help women in STEM relaunch post-career break, bias training for leaders and hiring managers are all examples of measures to bring about system-level changes.

Next, as *Society* plays an important role in nourishing inequity, often through social expectations of gender roles and societal stereotypes, it is important to create awareness and empower the community to recognise this and act. Examples of gender stereotypes include men being better at math and engineering than girls, girls being pretty, and boys being intelligent. An example of social expectation is women being the primary care provider for children and the elderly. Many more such stereotypes and expectations require tremendous social effort to create awareness and action.

Lastly, while *System* and *Society* level changes are most important, let's acknowledge that it will take time. I believe any change needs to begin from within, the *Self*, simply because each one of us has the power to be an agent of change.

As I began to face the consequence of my choice between life and career, self-doubt and self-sabotage grew within me, nourished by a victim mindset. Fortunately, I recognised these inner demons through self-awareness from the coaching support I sought out and became more aware of these very common issues and biases through my involvement in the women in science groups. This empowered me to find my courageous old self within, speak up for women in STEM, and lead initiatives to bring awareness and instigate action.

If there's one thing I would like my peers to hear, it is "You are enough". Do recognise that your brilliance and hard work have got you where you are, not just luck. Many of us hardly acknowledge our hard work or celebrate the small wins as we strive for more.

I fell victim to inequity. I blamed others. I blamed the system. I blamed society. I blamed myself. It was a negative cycle, which took conscious effort to escape.

I have still not accepted inequity, but I now know how to deal with it. I found a way; I found my way. Today, I no longer question "why I did my PhD" as I recognise my purpose. I feel immensely fulfilled as a speaker and coach serving people in STEM fields, tying together my 20 years of experience in the field and the skills I learnt and earned along the way. I urge you to reflect on your journey, applaud your accomplishments, and strategise how to thread it all together to showcase your best self.

Also, become aware of what your expectations are from yourself. Do not beat yourself up striving for perfection or have expectations to give 100% to every aspect of your life. It is humanly impossible to be a superwoman. Appreciate your unique journey, and never compare yourself with others. Finally, reach out to mentors, identify role models, lean in on peer support, and learn to delegate tasks.

ABOUT THE AUTHOR

DR LAKSHMI RAMACHANDRAN

Dr Lakshmi Ramachandran is a Keynote Speaker, and ICF-certified Coach focused on developing early career professionals in Science, Technology, Engineering and Mathematics (STEM) fields as effective future-ready leaders. She has a doctorate in Cell and Molecular Biology and spent 20 years in diverse science careers such as academic and industry research, science communication and research programme management before pivoting to the leadership and professional development space.

Dr Ramachandran attributes her passion to support women in STEM to her own career journey marked by multiple challenges such as career breaks, career reinvention and self-doubt, which she navigated through resilience, adaptability and self-awareness.

She is the Co-Founder of the Enoughness Mindset coaching and training programme, enabling high achievers and leaders to overcome the imposter syndrome and achieve a state of self-adequacy.

Dr Lakshmi lives in Singapore with her husband and two young boys. She has published an award-winning memoir cookbook, Roomies/Foodies.

You can connect with Dr Lakshmi at:

Speaker profile on KeyNoteWomen.com:
https://keynotewomen.com/speaker/lakshmi-ramachandran

✉ : mail.lakshmir@gmail.com

in : https://www.linkedin.com/in/drlakshmispeaks/

STORY SIXTEEN

The Equity Advantage – The Gateway to Possibilities, Potential and Profit

---

These actions require little effort other than mindfulness.

As someone passionate about DEI (Diversity, Equity and Inclusion) and speaking regularly at DEI and IWD (International Women's Day) events, as well as facilitating workshops for women leaders, I have always wondered why the progress made on this front is not proportional to the number and decibel level of conversations that happen.

So much so that every such event I attend, facilitate or speak at leaves me with a strong sense of déjà vu. And it is not surprising; a study by Boston Consulting Group[69] on gender diversity revealed that 91% of companies had a programme, and only 27% of women said they had benefited.

This is even though the business case for DEI has never been stronger. Some studies highlight that a diverse workforce leads to increased profitability, innovation, and engagement, amongst other equally valuable benefits:

- A Boston Consulting Group[70] report shows that companies with more diverse management teams have 19% higher revenue due to innovation.
- A McKinsey[71] study spanning 15 countries and over 1,000 large companies reveals that gender-diverse

---

[69]Rocio, L., Voigt, N., Tsusaka, M., Krentz, M. and Abouzahr, K. (Jan 23, 2018). "How Diverse Leadership Teams Boost Innovation". *BCG.* https://www.bcg.com/publications/2018/how-diverse-leadership-teams-boost-innovation. (accessed February 12, 2023).

[70]Rocio, L., et al. *ibid.*

[71]Dixon-Fyle, S., Dolan, K, Hunt, Dame V. and Prince, S. (May 19, 2020). *Diversity wins: How inclusion matters. McKinsey & Company.* https://www.mckinsey.com/featured-insights/diversity-and-inclusion/diversity-wins-how-inclusion-matters. (accessed February 12, 2023).

executive teams are 25% more likely to have above-average profitability. Furthermore, when it comes to ethnic and cultural diversity, their findings are equally compelling.

Executive teams with high ethnic and cultural diversity outperform those with low ethnic and cultural diversity by 36% in profitability. This was reinforced by another study by Deloitte[72], which also established that companies with diverse and inclusive workforces were 35% more likely to have financial returns above their industry median.

- Patagonia, a Great Place to Work awardee, is an excellent example of what DEI can do for your organisation. With roughly US$ 1 billion in sales and 3,000 employees worldwide, this outdoor clothing retailer prioritises advancing DEI within the company and engaging under-represented individuals and communities in the outdoor space and environmental movement.

  With 61%[73] of their workforce made up of millennials, a job-hopping generation according to a Gallup report[74]

---

[72]Bourke, J. and Dillon, B. (2018.) "The diversity and inclusion revolution, eight powerful truths". *Deloitte Review.* https://www2.deloitte.com/content/dam/insights/us/articles/4209_Diversity-and-inclusion-revolution/DI_Diversity-and-inclusion-revolution.pdf. (accessed February 12, 2023).

[73]Great Place to Work. (July 2019). "Working at Patagonia". https://www.greatplacetowork.com/certified-company/1000745. (accessed February 12, 2023).

[74]Adkins, A. (n.d.). "Millennials: The Job-Hopping Generation". *Gallup Business Journal.* https://www.gallup.com/workplace/231587/millennials-job-hopping-generation.aspx. (accessed February 12, 2023).

Patagonia has an impressive annual employee turnover rate of just 4%. These are numbers every business and HR leader would kill for. In fact, in 2019, the company's Head of HR, Dean Carter[75], jokingly remarked to the audience at a Talent Connect conference, "I call us the Hotel California – you check in, but you do not check out".

He revealed that at Patagonia, the talent acquisition team reads a resume from the bottom up to focus on the candidate's interests, activities and volunteer work. Why? Because, according to him, they are hiring human beings, not someone based on their education, ethnicity, race or economic background.

Their annual internship programmes, with no advertising, apart from posting it on their website, receives more than 9,000 applicants who are vying for just 17 internship spots.

Statistics aside, in my decades-plus experience working with HR professionals and business leaders, the most common gripes I hear are: "How can we keep our employees engaged? How do we attract the best talent and retain our top talent in today's competitive job market? How can I make my organisation a great place to work?"

---

[75]Anderson, B.M. (September 27, 2019). "5 'Ridiculous' Ways Patagonia Has Build a Culture That Does Well and Does Good". *LinkedIn*. https://www.linkedin.com/business/talent/blog/talent-connect/ways-patagonia-built-ridiculous-culture. (accessed February 12, 2023).

More often than not, I have pointed them at the Patagonia experience, which makes it obvious that DEI initiatives can be used to attract, engage, and retain talent.

Imagine if you have a long pipeline of talent desperate to join your organisation without having to lift a finger. A self-motivated and passionate workforce with a less than 4% turnover, who can't wait to come to work? Inspiring thought, isn't it? How could we make this happen?

We should also acknowledge that many organisations assume that their work on DEI is done once they have hired a diverse group of people who look different or achieved their diversity goals when they have the right representation at the leadership level. This is not true. To quote Fadzi Whande, a global diversity and inclusion strategist, "You can have diversity without inclusion and equity, or vice versa".

So, when we evolve our action plan, we must clearly understand that diversity is a crucial step. Still, an equal focus MUST accompany it on inclusion and equity to create a workplace where all employees feel safe, respected, valued and treated equitably because inclusion and equity truly unlock the full potential of diversity.

Keeping that in view, if I were to break it down, it isn't that we haven't made any progress on DEI. Progress HAS been made on diversity. However, because equity and inclusion got overlooked or did not get the attention they deserved, the true potential of DEI remained unlocked.

While speaking at one such DEI event recently, I asked this question to my audience, "What is ONE SIMPLE ACTION that YOU commit to taking on this front?"

The answers were plentiful. They left me more inspired than I felt in a long time. I decided to share them on every platform so that more people would be inclined to walk this talk, and DEI would become a part of our daily habits. Thus, we could start moving the needle on equity and inclusion in the workplace.

So what can we do about it at the workplace?

At the organisational level, leaders can help to foster an equitable and inclusive culture by taking these three steps:

1. **Build a culture of team trust and psychological safety** by doing simple things like having a process to ensure Everyone's voice is heard and respected in any structured workplace interaction.

   For example, one of the companies we work with has a process to ensure Everyone's voice is heard during team meetings; they allocate a couple of minutes to each person to share their views, starting with the junior most person.

   The sales team of another company developed a team social contract that clearly outlines the rules of engagement with other team members. Their team's social contract had a list of six behaviours, which had been agreed upon by all team members. These actions require little effort other than mindfulness.

They evolved such a simple yet powerful social contract and laid out a pragmatic protocol to call out anyone who breached the social contract and demonstrated toxic behaviours.

Now, that's an important piece of the puzzle because I worked with another client who shared her experience of speaking up at a team meeting. The senior leader had tabled an issue and requested everyone to speak their mind. She bravely shared her honest opinion, but the senior leader responded angrily, stating she didn't fully understand the issue. After that incident, my client was too intimidated to speak up again. Such active disengagement usually results in people eventually exiting the organisation.

But here's the good news: when leaders can increase team psychological safety by fostering a culture of trust, amazing things happen! According to the Harvard Business Review[76], organisations with high trust levels result in 66% closer relationships between colleagues, 41% less depersonalisation and an 11% increase in empathy.

When trust is high, we naturally create an environment where we can understand and appreciate each other's unique experiences and promote inclusivity and equity in the workplace. A diverse workforce is only truly

---

[76]Zak, P.J. (2017). "The Neuroscience of Trust- Management behaviours that foster employee engagement". *Harvard Business Review.* https://hbr.org/2017/01/the-neuroscience-of-trust. (accessed February 12, 2023).

valuable if individuals from diverse backgrounds feel acknowledged, valued and heard.

2. **Conduct regular assessments of policies, processes and practices to identify areas of bias and inequity.** This allows leaders to ensure their DEI practices are in tune with current realities and anomalies are regularly identified and removed.

   Take the example of one of the KPMG businesses we have been working with. They conducted a study to deepen their understanding of social inequalities in their workplace. Through that study, they discovered that socioeconomic background (measured by parental occupation) substantially affects career progression compared to any other diversity characteristic. Individuals from lower socio-economic backgrounds took an average 19%[77] longer to progress to the next grade. So the firm committed to increasing its leaders from low socio-economic backgrounds to 29% by 2030. Accordingly, they launched promotional readiness programmes for high-potential employees from underrepresented groups.

   The result? 25% of KPMG's partners now come from low socio-economic backgrounds, employees from ethnic minorities and women have faster career progression, and the company is thriving.

[77]KPMG UK. (December 2022). *Social Mobility Progression Report 2022: Mind the Gap.* https://kpmg.com/uk/en/home/media/press-releases/2022/12/social-class-is-the-biggest-barrier-to-career-progression.html. (accessed February 12, 2023).

Patagonia approaches its policies with a unique perspective; they give much more weight to their impact on their employees' lives than traditional measures such as productivity and engagement.

According to Dean Cater, 100% of women on the company's paid maternity leave return to work compared to the industry average of 25-30% who leave their jobs after giving birth. Male employees are also offered paid paternity leave, which means that childcare doesn't rest solely on the woman.

And that is the point I wish to highlight; equitable and inclusive policies level the playing field for men and women in terms of advancement and opportunities.

3. **Ensure leadership accountability and capabilities for DEI** by ensuring equity and inclusion are reflected in their scorecards. Ensure adequate training support is provided to managers at all levels, particularly middle managers. For example, equipping them with the tools and skills to navigate tricky conversations without putting their foot in their mouth, i.e. knowing what to say and do as well as what not to say and do.

   One international bank we worked with put 24 women leaders through a six-month comprehensive training programme to increase the number of women leaders at the senior leadership level.

The three steps listed above are not exhaustive since every company is different, and there is no one-size-fits-all approach to DEI. What's most important to keep in mind is ensuring we're giving EQUAL attention to diversity, equity and inclusion.

But here's the secret sauce: the real game-changer for equity and inclusion is when each one of us takes personal responsibility. Granted, inclusive policies and practices do help the cause, but our actions taken every day and in every interaction will create that big, seismic shift.

Simply put – DEI is not just HR's job, our manager's job or the DEI leader's job – it's all of our jobs.

When my spouse was suddenly posted to Dubai by his company, I felt I had only two choices. One, leave my job and go with my husband or two, keep my job and leave my husband in Dubai. When I shared my dilemma with him, he said something that changed my perspective "Why do you see this as a binary choice? Have you considered that there could be a third possibility, perhaps a temporary assignment for you in Dubai? Have you considered asking them?"

Almost instinctively, I felt a push back within myself and immediately came up with a myriad of reasons why it was impossible. I was still sceptical when I reached the office the following day, but I mustered the courage and asked.

To my surprise, my manager said, "Sure, why not?" We Don't have an opening for you in Dubai but let me discuss this with HR so that you can work part of the time in Singapore, and the other amount of the time in Dubai, working remotely. (Bear in mind that this was before COVID-19.)

When he suggested that, I was surprised that this option had emerged. It hadn't even occurred to me. Three months later, I moved to Dubai, and my boss, teammates and family rallied around me to make this arrangement work.

This experience showed me that DEI requires a collective effort, with every person playing a crucial role. I have an open-minded spouse who made me aware of how I was limiting my choices because of my beliefs, a supportive boss and company that came up with a flexible work arrangement, and my newfound courage to step up and ask for what I needed.

Like my story, when we all embrace DEI in our personal lives, it positively spills over to our professional lives and transforms our workplace cultures.

Here are three ways to help us:

1. **Be aware of your attitudes, behaviours and biases** by pausing to reflect when your values and beliefs are being challenged and be open to feedback. It may sound scary, but exploring your conscious and unconscious biases can help you become more self-aware and take necessary action.

   Fadzi Whande[78] shared in her TEDx talk that even with the best intentions, she had excluded connecting with white men she believed were privileged and therefore

---

[78]Whande, F. (n.d.). "How Diversity Heaven can be Inclusion Hell". *TEDxPerth.* https://www.ted.com/talks/fadzi_whande_how_diversity_heaven_can_be_inclusion_hell. (accessed February 12, 2023).

did not require her to understand them. They were the ones who needed to understand the marginalised. But she soon realised that true inclusiveness means making space for everyone, regardless of their background.

One of my coaching clients shared that the women's chapter at his workplace kept their events exclusively ladies-only, and the only men invited were usually senior leaders. He opined that if men could participate, it would help them gain a deeper insight into what their female colleagues were going through. That way, he would know what to do to improve things.

So, in that spirit of inclusivity, let's invite everyone to the conversation – we all benefit from more people being educated on DEI issues and becoming more self-aware.

2. **Tackle bias by calling it out at home or the workplace**
   My brother and I were cleaning up after dinner at a recent family dinner party, and my two aunts made their way into the kitchen. They were amazed to see my brother washing the dishes, and one of them exclaimed, "Wow, you're such a good boy for helping your mum like this".

   I couldn't resist and turned around, "Excuse me, what about me? How come I never get any praise when you see me washing the dishes!" My aunts blushed, and one of them chuckled and said, "You're also a good girl!"

   This may seem like a trivial incident to some, but remember that such events are responsible for creating the centuries-old bias that we are now struggling to overcome.

3. **Talk DEI with everyone you know**

   Find that opportunity to chat all things DEI with your parents, spouse, kids, relatives, and friends. It's a great way to raise awareness and ensure future generations aren't stuck with the same biases we may have had growing up.

The road to a more equitable and inclusive world may seem like an arduous marathon, but every tiny step towards DEI brings us closer to a world where equity and inclusiveness are just how things are done.

As Lao Tzu wisely said, "A journey of a thousand miles starts with a single step". So let's take that first step together today.

ABOUT THE AUTHOR

WENDY LEONG

Wendy Leong is a learning and organisational development professional, speaker, facilitator and coach passionate about helping people harness their potential and perform at their best.

Wendy has over two decades of sales, marketing, and talent development expertise working with iconic companies like Procter & Gamble, The Body Shop and Olympus. Recognised for her mastery in talent development initiatives, Wendy was awarded the Procter & Gamble CEO Award, bestowed to global top performers.

As an experienced facilitator who can engage multicultural audiences, Wendy has delivered transformational keynotes and global workshops.

Wendy is the Summit Director of Rise Through the Ranks, a global online leadership conference that has reached out to thousands of executives from over 70 countries and is currently the Head of Strategic Solutions at Influence

Solutions, an award-winning organisational development firm with a global footprint that helps companies to create high-trust cultures.

You can connect with Wendy at:

Speaker profile on KeyNoteWomen.com:
https://www.keynotewomen.com/speaker/wendy-leong

✉ : wendy@influence-solutions.com

in : https://www.linkedin.com/in/wendyleongconnects/

STORY SEVENTEEN

Mind the Equity Gap

Get comfortable with being uncomfortable.

Meritocracy, Identity, and Privilege

"Where is your accent from?" I often hear from new colleagues and acquaintances.

Having lived and worked in five different countries and within two regions, I hear a version of this question frequently. Generally, people are curious to learn about my heritage and do it respectfully. But at times, it sounds more like: "Wow, you are so articulate, but you are not an English native speaker. Where are you actually from?" This is when I pause to wonder whether they realise their question has an exclusionary and stereotyping effect.

My name is Magda. I am a Diversity, Equity, and Inclusion practitioner with 18 years of professional experience. I am Polish, white, female, cisgender, heterosexual, non-disabled, neurotypical, middle-class, and university-educated, a parent, a caregiver, a millennial and a bilingual English and Polish speaker. My social identity grants me certain privileges in various settings, albeit to different degrees. However, certain facets of my identity have been sources of bias and inequity.

When I was young, my mother always said, "Study and work hard, and you will succeed in whatever you choose to pursue". Fast forward a few years, I often hear statements such as: "You have such neat handwriting. Can you please take notes and share the minutes?" and from a manager during an annual performance review: "Magda, you are a great girl, and I want you to succeed in this organization". Or the frequent question around my accent and nationality when delivered with a stereotypical undertone.

Was my mother right? Does meritocracy allow everyone to progress with dignity, respect, and equity? Unfortunately, the answer is no, not everyone. Historically, vast global systemic and institutional inequities favour individuals with privileged identities while neglecting the marginalised groups who continue to experience exclusion and discrimination in various areas of their personal and professional lives. It is important to add that anyone can, intentionally or not, create inequity and make discriminatory statements or decisions, and it is not specific to any identity.

Education, hard work, creative ideas, and model citizenship behaviours do not necessarily equate to workplace development, advancement, and respect.

Nevertheless, my own experience of inequity and exclusion brought me closer to my journey towards Diversity, Equity, and Inclusion (DEI) as I wanted to understand the historical context of this area of work and learn how to improve structural and behavioural equity.

Diversity, Equity, and Inclusion

"Why are you interested in a position in DEI?" I was once asked in a job interview.

I was blessed to have the opportunity to travel internationally with choirs and music groups during my primary and secondary years of music education. Meeting students from different cultures and communicating using foreign languages was exhilarating.

This early appreciation of diversity led me to study English at university, hoping I could turn the thrill of multicultural interactions into a career. After further studies in Human Resources, tourism, executive coaching, and a relocation to Asia, I started my DEI journey at a multinational organisation in Singapore.

I have found great fulfilment in DEI because it bridges business, people, and organisational culture while providing opportunities for diverse interactions, learning, and, above all, building equity.

Through 18 years of my DEI practice, I can see that historically marginalised communities still experience bias, exclusion, and discrimination as organisations struggle to equip their workforce with tools to create equitable and inclusive work environments. While organisations provide policies, benefits, and standards towards structural equity, this does not translate to behavioural equity. I am yet to see an organisation that has successfully closed this gap, as people with marginalised backgrounds continue to report exclusion, discrimination and bias from their managers, senior leaders, and colleagues.

Structural and Behavioural Equity

Let's look closely at structural and behavioural equity concepts. Structural or organisational equity is the distribution of power and resources and whether that distribution leads to equitable outcomes and growth opportunities for all employees[79].

[79]Mahin, S. and Rosenberg, S. (February 24, 2021). "Organizational Equity: Your Missing Metric for Success". *Kenan Institute of Private Enterprise.* https://kenaninstitute.unc.edu/kenan-insight/organizational-equity-your-missing-metric-for-success/ (accessed February 10, 2023).

Examples include organisational policies, employee lifecycle processes, public statements and commitments, evidence-based workforce diversity reporting, diversity targets, equity baselines, formal equity and inclusion programmes, and benefits focused on diverse populations. Organisations are legally required to create minimum standards to meet the needs of protected groups or social identities from harassment and discrimination, which is a requirement that differs from country to country.

Behavioural equity is an activation of the systems and their fair implementation leading to citizenship behaviour where individuals exceed organisational expectations. Conversely, the lack of behavioural equity, meaning fair processes, respect, and rewards, can result in moral disengagement, de-motivation, and decreased productivity[80].

Leaders and managers activate equity through respectful relationships, fair treatment of people, and equitable distribution of power, resources, and opportunities. Other examples include inviting diverse perspectives, welcoming respectful conflict, avoiding judgement, calling out bias and discrimination, identifying and acknowledging knowledge gaps, and learning about different social identities.

I will share a few examples from my professional experience to help us examine the gap between structural and behavioural equity and discuss possible solutions and strategies to

---

[80]Zoghbi-Manrique-de-Lara, P. (July 2010). "Do Unfair Procedures Predict Employees' Ethical Behavior by Deactivating Formal Regulations?" *Springer.* jstor.org/stable/40784702. (accessed February 10, 2023).

minimise this gap. Let's dive in.

Organisations, Managers, and Equity

"I am finally going to do it, Magda. I can finally transition. I have been waiting for it for so long," Stella* exclaimed, throwing her arms around my neck.

She had been promoted to a senior role in a multinational bank and felt secure enough to proceed with a life-long dream of gender affirmation surgery. She has been open about her gender identity at work for several years, although not everyone in the organisation has embraced it.

She experienced strange looks, inappropriate jokes, and many toilet-related arguments at work, but she chose to focus on her work and targets. Her perseverance and hard work led to a promotion and a validation of her status within the organisation. Stella reached out to Human Resources (HR). She was pleasantly surprised to hear that she was eligible for benefits such as financial support for her hormone replacement therapy, gender affirmation surgery, and additional leave. She was ecstatic.

A few days later, she met with her manager and discussed her intention to transition with him. He was familiar with Stella's identity but was completely unaware of the company policy and benefits structure around gender affirmation. He frowned, crossed his arms, and asked how much time off she would need to take and who would pick up her work while away. She assured him that her performance would not be impacted as she would provide ample notice of any absences.

In the next few weeks, he changed her client roster and did not allocate as many new clients to her as before. Stella was often spoken over in meetings, excluded from social gatherings, and felt isolated from the team, disengaged, and discriminated against. Stella reported her manager's conduct to HR, but he did not change his attitude or behaviour until he moved on to a new role in a different company.

In Stella's situation, there was a clear gap between structural and behavioural equity as her manager did not successfully activate structural equity created to support transgender employees. Managers should proactively build their capabilities and inclusive leadership skills to minimise the equity gap, provide the expected duty of care, and meet the diverse needs of their teams. It is a learning journey; however, anyone can improve their behavioural equity and create sustainable and inclusive leadership capabilities with intention, practice, and reflection.

A Tale of Two Managers

"I was going to assign you a new project, Magda. But I thought you were busy, so I asked another team member to take it on," my female line manager told me while I was working in a multinational company in Singapore. She was one of my two managers at the time, as I handled two portfolios.

As I was pregnant with my second child, I thought to myself that she was being considerate, but on second thought, I realised she was discriminatory. I leaned back and wondered: did she just say it out loud? While I reported to her, she excluded me from the project meetings I was involved in and delegated her administrative duties to me, which were not part of my scope of work. She mocked my English while giving me feedback on tasks such as minute-taking. She was a toxic and exclusionary manager whose actions and comments expressed a discriminatory attitude towards me. She was not invested in my professional growth and success within the organisation.

My second manager, on the other hand, was a fantastic mentor who empowered and inspired me to bring my authentic self to work. She asked me about my long-term career aspirations, gave tips on getting there, delegated complex stretch assignments, and included me in formal and informal meetings of her broader department. She obtained a budget from the global team to sponsor half of my salary from the company headquarters and provided me with leadership visibility across global teams.

She invited me to the global portfolio strategy summit in the United States while I was six months pregnant. She was an inclusive manager who celebrated my social identity and was invested in my growth, learning and visibility.

Although both managers were women and young mothers, they created very different work experiences for me within the same organisation. One created an equity gap and made me feel excluded, invisible, and underappreciated, while the latter enhanced my experience and made me feel valued, appreciated, and included. Everyone is responsible for leading interactions with respect, empathy, and equity. Managers who are authentic allies and speak up for anyone with less privilege add tremendous value to any organisation, as they positively contribute to building equitable work cultures.

We all have Inherent Biases

"Why does she want to meet with me? We have nothing in common other than we are in the same department. What are we going to talk about?" I wondered, having received a lunch meeting invitation from a colleague from the Management Associate Programme.

This was during my early years after relocating to Singapore, a melting pot of ethnic cultures and religious traditions. As a Polish, Catholic, and white woman, I wondered why she wanted to meet me. She was an Indian and Muslim, and my knowledge and understanding of her cultural background were limited at the time.

When feeling discomfort around my colleague's cultural background, I realised I was experiencing bias based on the fear of the unknown. What if I say the wrong thing? I should have strong cultural literacy; I am a DEI practitioner. Then, it struck me: no one is immune to inequitable reactions and biases. We grow up in a specific culture, and it becomes a frame of reference for understanding and evaluating other cultures. Over time, we develop an ethnocentric and incomplete view of the world, and it is easier to default to the culture we know and feel comfortable with. Any new culture will require curiosity and a certain level of discomfort until we have direct experience interacting with persons from that culture and build our awareness.

Consequently, I decided to take my own advice: put my curiosity hat on and face my discomfort head-on. During our lunch meeting, we both had an amazing experience learning about each other's cultural heritage and identities. Despite our vast cultural differences, we discovered that we had similar views on personal values, family, health, and lifestyle. We became fast friends, met outside work to discover multicultural Singapore, and I attended her wedding in India after she moved back to her home country. To this day, we are still in touch.

Recognising this gap in my equity and inclusion practice taught me to be open and unafraid of embracing the unknown and meeting people from different cultures and backgrounds. Furthermore, it helped me improve my self-awareness and build an appreciation of a new culture, demonstrating that interactions with diverse populations help minimise the equity gap. This situation of facing my own bias inspired me to create a new habit of meeting at least one person every month with an identity different from mine to continue improving my cultural intelligence. We need to get comfortable with being uncomfortable to learn, expand our horizons, and build meaningful connections with people from different social identities.

Mind the Equity Gap

Building structural equity is an orchestrated effort that requires everyone in an organisation to get involved. Meanwhile, we can improve the behavioural equity around us by creating an environment of trust, psychological safety, awareness of diverse social identities, and genuine empathy and care. This applies not only to leaders or managers. Every person should have equity and inclusion goals to improve one's equity literacy and capabilities.

Here are three tips to help embrace equity:

1. **Learn:** Use existing online and organisational resources to understand various facets of difference, build empathy, and manage your own biases. Learn about different social identities, issues different marginalised groups face and how they show up in your country, company, and social circles. Attend events periodically on topics you disagree with or do not understand to learn and stretch yourself. Equity is not about agreeing with everyone and disregarding your values or viewpoints but an opportunity to respectfully disagree while honouring your identity.
2. **Connect:** Diversify your social networks, as we usually spend time with people with similar backgrounds. Reach out to diverse individuals in your personal and professional circles, get to know them, ask questions, and expand your knowledge. Make weekly or monthly meaningful connections with diverse friends or colleagues and learn to face your own biases, persist despite the discomfort, and learn to embrace the risks of the unknown. Lead all interactions with respect in mind and, when unsure, ask questions from a place of curiosity.
3. **Lead:** Know your teams well and distribute resources,

tasks, and opportunities equitably. Be an authentic ally and speak up for others with less privilege, even when they are not in the room. Create a safe space for open communication and call out bias safely. Encourage diverse perspectives and respectful conflict. Diverse perspectives fuel creativity and more innovative solutions. Mentor someone from different social identities and role-model equity in how you interact with others.

We are all responsible for creating an equitable and inclusive environment around us, so treat people the way they want to be treated. I hope my experiences and stories help you reflect that we can bring everyone along on the journey towards equity through lifelong learning, commitment, connection, and accepting discomfort.

Let's walk the talk on closing the equity gap together.

**Names have been changed.*

ABOUT THE AUTHOR

MAGDALENA POULIN

Magdalena Poulin is a recognised expert on Diversity, Equity, and Inclusion with extensive experience building global and regional strategies for multinational organisations.She helps organisations create inclusive cultures and systemic and sustainable changes.

She frequently speaks on transforming organisations and teams through active allyship, belonging, mentorship, change management, inclusive leadership, intersectionality and creating shared value.

Her international career, culturally diverse family and experiences of exclusion stemming from an intersection of her cultural heritage, linguistic background, gender, age, family, and caregiver status, inspire her keynotes and provide a catalyst for social change.

Magdalena designed Diversity & Inclusion strategies and large-scale programmes at AIG, HP, and EMC and is currently based at Macquarie University in Sydney, Australia.

She is a co-founding member of KeyNote Women, she leads the KeyNote Oceania chapter and volunteers at a Polish Community Language School in Sydney.

You can connect with Magdalena at:

Speaker profile on KeyNoteWomen.com:
https://www.keynotewomen.com/speaker/magdalena-poulin

: https://www.linkedin.com/in/magdalenapoulin/

: https://www.internationalwomensday.com/Speaker/1462/Magdalena-Poulin

Call for Support

KeyNote Women Speakers is on a mission to bring more diversity to speaking stages.

We are a community committed to amplifying women's voices – on stage, at work, and in private. In addition to our online directory and being a community where experts and thought leaders can sharpen their skills and enjoy peer support, we have a training programme to provide less experienced public speakers with the mindset and skills to impact from the stage.

We operate as a non-profit and want to make an even more significant dent. This requires funding. Organisations can support us by engaging our speakers, considering our highly effective speaker training and coaching programme, or with charitable donations and sponsorship of our upcoming events and book series.

Contact Info@KeyNoteWomen.com to arrange a discussion with our leadership team to explore how you can get involved!

Acknowledgement

This book took a lot of people through a rollercoaster of emotions. We couldn't have done it without the help of the amazing project leader, author, diplomat and mental support provider Sara Kelly. Maneesha Benedict leant in throughout the project to ensure that we got everything across the finishing line in time. Leslie Caoile is our faithful support at KeyNote Women in all matters, and also this book. A special shout out to Melanie Voskamp and Karine Lespinasse who volunteered their time to read and review our authors' chapters. We appreciate the authors' patience and speediness in delivering their inspirational stories. A big "thank you"! to the marketing team consisting of Suralini Madawela and Yensuthantharasenan Yensegera as well as Varsha Rathi who are promoting the authors. Without our more than 150 speakers, volunteers, clients and partners, there wouldn't even be a KeyNote - we appreciate every single one of you. And finally the publishers, Global Influencers Publishing House (Neera Gupta and Shikha Sarkar), are wonderful and mission-driven people, dedicated to delivering even with impossible deadlines. Couldn't have done it without all of you wonderful people!

Thank you.

Mette Johansson
Founder and Chair of KeyNote Women Speakers

Made in the USA
Las Vegas, NV
17 April 2023

70710679R00159